SINGAPORE AND MULTILATERAL GOVERNANCE
SECURING OUR FUTURE

IPS-NATHAN LECTURES

SINGAPORE AND MULTILATERAL GOVERNANCE

SECURING OUR FUTURE

NOELEEN HEYZER

Published by

World Scientific Publishing Co. Pte. Ltd.
5 Toh Tuck Link, Singapore 596224
USA office: 27 Warren Street, Suite 401-402, Hackensack, NJ 07601
UK office: 57 Shelton Street, Covent Garden, London WC2H 9HE

National Library Board, Singapore Cataloguing in Publication Data
Name(s): Heyzer, Noeleen.
Title: Singapore and multilateral governance : securing our future / Noeleen Heyzer.
Other Title(s): IPS-Nathan Lectures.
Description: Singapore : World Scientific Publishing Co. Pte. Ltd., [2023]
Identifier(s): ISBN 978-981-12-6326-2 (hardcover) | 978-981-12-6417-7 (paperback) |
    978-981-12-6327-9 (ebook for institutions) | 978-981-12-6328-6 (ebook for individuals)
Subject(s): LCSH: Singapore--Foreign relations--21st century. |
    Singapore--Politics and government--21st century.
Classification: DDC 327.5957--dc23

British Library Cataloguing-in-Publication Data
A catalogue record for this book is available from the British Library.

Copyright © 2023 by Noeleen Heyzer & Institute of Policy Studies

All rights reserved.

For any available supplementary material, please visit
https://www.worldscientific.com/worldscibooks/10.1142/13052#t=suppl

Desk Editor: Lai Ann

Typeset by Stallion Press
Email: enquiries@stallionpress.com

THE S R NATHAN FELLOWSHIP FOR THE STUDY OF SINGAPORE

AND THE IPS-NATHAN LECTURE SERIES

The S R Nathan Fellowship for the Study of Singapore was established by the Institute of Policy Studies (IPS) in 2013 to support research on public policy and governance issues. With the generous contributions of individual and corporate donors, and a matching government grant, IPS raised around S$5.9 million to endow the Fellowship.

Each S R Nathan Fellow, appointed under the Fellowship, delivers a series of IPS-Nathan Lectures during his or her term. These public lectures aim to promote public understanding and discourse on issues of critical national interest.

The Fellowship is named after Singapore's sixth and longest-serving President, the late S R Nathan, in recognition of his lifetime of service to Singapore.

IPS-Nathan Lectures

Print ISSN: 2630-4996
Online ISSN: 2630-5003

Published:

Vol. 10: *Singapore and Multilateral Governance: Securing Our Future*
by Noeleen Heyzer

Vol. 9: *The Singapore Synthesis: Innovation, Inclusion, Inspiration*
by Ravi Menon

Vol. 8: *Gender Equality: The Time Has Come*
by Corinna Lim

Vol. 7: *World in Transition: Singapore's Future*
by Chan Heng Chee

Vol. 6: *The Idea of Singapore: Smallness Unconstrained*
by Tan Tai Yong

Vol. 5: *Seeking a Better Urban Future*
by Cheong Koon Hean

Vol. 4: *Can Singapore Fall?: Making the Future for Singapore*
by Lim Siong Guan

Vol. 3: *The Challenges of Governance in a Complex World*
by Peter Ho

Vol. 2: *Dealing with an Ambiguous World*
by Bilahari Kausikan

Vol. 1: *The Ocean in a Drop Singapore: The Next Fifty Years*
by Ho Kwon Ping

CONTENTS

Foreword	ix
About the Moderators	xv
About the Cover Illustrator	xvii

Lecture I — Grand Transitions: Our Multilateral Journey	**1**
The Multilateral Moment	2
"Guardian of the Charter": Successes and Failures	5
Solidarity as Self-Interest	19
Question-and-Answer Session	23
Moderator: Mr Ho Kwon Ping	

Lecture II — Great Disruptions: The Struggle for Our Normative Future	**35**
Four Great Disruptions	37
Rethinking Sustainable Recovery in the COVID-19 World	41
Normative Struggles for Our Future	43
Seizing the Opportunity for Change	46
Question-and-Answer Session	58
Moderator: Professor Tommy Koh	

Lecture III — Securing Our Future: A Renewed Multilateralism   69
  The Foundation of Our Global Future   71
  Networked-Inclusive-Effective Multilateralism   77
  Securing Singapore's Future: An Epicentre of Multilateralism?   81
  Conclusion   87
  Question-and-Answer Session   89
  Moderator: Professor Chan Heng Chee

Bibliography   99
Index   105

FOREWORD

Dr Noeleen Heyzer speaking at the second lecture of her IPS-Nathan Lecture series
Source: Jacky Ho for the Institute of Policy Studies.

We are living now at a critical moment in the history of human civilisation, marked by great paradoxes. On the one hand, we are poised at the pinnacle of human creative energy, with monumental achievements of the human mind, body and spirit. Yet at the same time, we wield unparalleled powers of destruction — too many lives are still devastated by war, conflict, displacement and poverty, while unsustainable development and lifestyles of overconsumption are dangerously disrupting the balance of our ecosystems. Our global landscape has become more interconnected than ever, due to economic integration and greater connectivity through technology; but we are also witnessing deeper fragmentation, characterised by eroded trust between people and systems that have failed to provide for the needs of the vulnerable.

The cataclysmic forces that threaten humanity today are the consequences of human actions and decisions. The very survival of humanity and our planet hinges upon the choices we make now, collectively and individually. As the naturalist David Attenborough reminds us:

> *We are at a unique stage in our history. Never before have we had such an awareness of what we are doing to the planet, and never before have we had the power to do something about that … the future of humanity and indeed, all life on earth, now depends on us.*[1]

If humanity is to overcome the seemingly insurmountable challenges of our times, we need to act decisively and collectively now, as a global community. The world is in urgent need of global leadership and coordinated global responses to an unprecedented global emergency, which constitutes the greatest threat to humanity since World War II (WWII). It is precisely at times like these that the leadership and values of multilateralism are needed. The foremost challenge for global leaders today is how to govern for social inclusion, sustainable growth and resilience. Our systems of global governance — encompassing international institutions as well as transnational grassroots networks — need to be constantly renewed and recalibrated in order to respond strategically and effectively to the specific needs and problems of humanity and the natural world.

In our present international order characterised by globalisation, fragmentation and disparities of power and wealth, how do we balance the complexities of geopolitical realism with the values of humanistic idealism? What are the core values that guide us, especially decision-makers in

---

[1] *Blue Planet II*, episode 7, "Our Blue Planet," presented by David Attenborough, aired December 10, 2017, on BBC, https://www.bbcearth.com/shows/blue-planet-ii.

governments and institutions, to practise governance for social inclusion and sustainability while upholding principles of justice and peaceful co-existence? Ideals are not simply a utopian dream; they are a constellation of guiding stars that can steer our governments and global institutions towards embodying and enacting our needs, hopes and aspirations for the greater common good. Formulated in the aftermath of WWII, the United Nations Charter is a prime example of a set of principles that still resonates with the realities of the world today. It emphasises the importance of multilateralism as an essential path of global governance and a necessary mechanism for achieving the pillars of peace and security, human rights, the rule of law and development.

The overall theme of my lecture series is "Singapore and Multilateral Governance: Securing Our Future". Singapore's past, present and future are highly dependent on and integrated with multilateral governance. As the only island city-state in the world, going alone and being isolated was never an option in our journey from third world to first. Singapore and Asia have benefited greatly from the rule-based multilateral global order that emerged after WWII — based on values, norms and institutions. In this three-part lecture series, I examine how Singapore can continue to contribute to multilateral governance amid 21st century global challenges. What does it mean for Singapore to engage with and revitalise this multilateral world? How can we build upon the kind of long-term vision and multilateral governance that historically brought giant leaps in our living standards and human development? And, critically, how can we secure our common future and shape what we become as a nation?

The first lecture, entitled "Grand Transitions: Our Multilateral Journey", focuses on where we have been and what experience we have come from. Grand transitions of the past and present continue to impact our future. The aftermath of WWII, the fall of the Berlin Wall, the 2008 Global Financial Crisis and, now, the global COVID-19 pandemic have all revealed fragilities in our world and region that require serious attention. Since our inception as a nation, our mindset, choices and partnerships have helped shape today's

Singapore. Our decisions in international cooperation, at regional and national levels, helped bring about prosperity and peace and create "Rising Asia". This lecture reflects on Singapore's journey in a multilateral world, examines the mindset of "solidarity as self-interest" and considers the need for multilateral governance to be continually informed by successes and failures in an evolving development landscape, in order to grapple with pivotal moments of transition. It also takes into account the frequent disconnect between norms of multilateral governance and the practice of development and corporate governance on the reality of people's lives.

The second lecture is on "Great Disruptions: The Struggle for Our Normative Future". Handling disruptions is the great test of our generation. Four great disruptions: health pandemic, climate crisis, the cyber world and conflicts in our interconnected but divided world are unprecedented. The interlocking disruptions are endangering the very safety and sustainability of human life, demanding new normative frameworks and arrangements in multilateral governance. Across the world we are witnessing struggles and social movements unfolding — notably of women and youth, rooted in community organising and strengthened by transnational solidarity — calling for effective action to address problems that matter most to our human future. I highlight the need to invest in the nexus of sustainable development, global health and human security as global public goods as we rethink sustainable recovery in the COVID-19 world. How do we fare amidst these struggles? Can Singapore be a key stakeholder for change in the multilateral world? I discuss Singapore's leadership in mobilising the concerns of medium and small states in the multilateral space, contributing to a normative future that is more equitable, inclusive and sustainable, and to a global community where more people can flourish.

The third lecture, entitled "Securing Our Future: A Renewed Multilateralism", focuses on our future. We are living through a time every bit as momentous as that faced by our forefathers and mothers seven decades ago. The framework of multilateral governance that has secured our present now needs to be renewed and strengthened to deal with the interlocking disruptions that threaten our future. Our generation is tasked with nothing less than the rejuvenation of the multilateral rule-based order to secure our future. We will be defined by how we respond to this call of destiny. As we look towards the future that our children will inherit, we must ask ourselves: What kind of world will we leave them? What kind of Singapore society do we want to become? What will be our role in and contribution to our common future? Can Singapore become an epicentre, a node for the new multilateralism and a model of enlightened self-preservation, committed to the stewardship of our global commons and public goods?

I would like to express my deepest gratitude to Institute of Policy Studies (IPS) Director Janadas Devan and the S R Nathan Fellowship Committee for appointing me as the 10th S R Nathan Fellow for the Study of Singapore. It is a great honour to be part of this distinguished Fellowship, remembering the legacy of former President of Singapore, S R Nathan, whose incredible resolve and ingenuity to overcome all odds is the story of so many of our pioneers. The late S R Nathan encapsulates the spirit and DNA of Singapore, unafraid to take control and shape our own destiny. Special thanks to the IPS team for their exceptional support: Eunice Amor Oh, my research assistant; Associate Director Liang Kaixin; Senior Executive Cai Dewei, and all the dedicated staff working behind the scenes. My heartfelt thanks go to Chairman Ho Kwon Ping, Professor Tommy Koh and Professor Chan Heng Chee for moderating the question-and-answer sessions of these lectures.

Finally, it is my hope that these lectures underscore the interconnectedness that defines our human condition. We are not isolated beings existing in atomised fragments of reality — we are beings nurtured by family, community, society, dependent on the wellbeing of others, and of the earth and the cosmos. This underlying interconnectedness and interdependence of existence means that destruction of one part of the whole inevitably entails repercussions for all. It is our responsibility as leaders to ensure a just and equitable system of global governance that uplifts humanity and safeguards the natural world. Responding to the challenges of our times, global leaders — governments, private sector and individuals — can either contribute to a "breakthrough" to usher in a more sustainable, safer future, or to a state of "breakdown" and ongoing, deepening crisis. Through multilateralism, let us strive to reimagine our world and realise the humanistic ideals so eloquently expressed by Nelson Mandela:

> *Let there be justice for all. Let there be peace for all. Let there be work, bread, water and salt for all. Let each know that for each the body, the mind and the soul have been freed to fulfil themselves.*[2]

Noeleen Heyzer

---

[2] South African Government, "Statement of the President of the African National Congress, Nelson Mandela, at his Inauguration as President of the Democratic Republic of South Africa, Union Buildings, Pretoria," May 10, 1994, https://www.gov.za/statement-president-african-national-congress-nelson-mandela-his-inauguration-president-democratic.

ABOUT THE MODERATORS

Ho Kwon Ping is Executive Chairman of Banyan Tree Holdings, Laguna Resorts and Hotels and Thai Wah Ltd, all of which are family-controlled but publicly listed on the Singapore and Thailand stock exchanges. For his public service as the founding Chairman of Singapore Management University (SMU), Mr Ho was awarded the Singapore government's Meritorious Service Medal (2009) and Distinguished Service Order (DSO). Mr Ho has also received honorary doctorates from Johnson & Wales University and Hong Kong Polytechnic University, and numerous industry awards. He has served on the boards of multinational companies such as Standard Chartered Bank plc. and Diageo plc. Mr Ho is married to Claire Chiang, who is Senior Vice President of Banyan Tree Holdings Limited. They have three children — two sons and a daughter.

Professor Tommy Koh is Ambassador-at-Large at the Ministry of Foreign Affairs and the Institute of Policy Studies' Special Adviser. At the National University of Singapore (NUS), he is Professor of Law, Chairman of the Governing Board of the Centre for International Law and previously Rector of Tembusu College. He is also Chairman of the Advisory Committee of the Master's Degree on Environmental Management at NUS. In his diplomatic career, he was Singapore's Permanent Representative to the United Nations (UN) in New York, Ambassador to the United States (US), High Commissioner to Canada and Ambassador to Mexico, as well as President of the Third UN Conference on the Law of the Sea. Professor Koh was also the UN Secretary-General's Special Envoy to Russia, Estonia, Latvia and Lithuania.

Professor Chan Heng Chee is Ambassador-at-Large at the Ministry of Foreign Affairs and Professor at the Lee Kuan Yew Centre for Innovative Cities at the Singapore University of Technology and Design (SUTD). Ambassador Chan is Chairman of the Board of Trustees at ISEAS-Yusof Ishak Institute (ISEAS), Deputy Chairman of the Social Science Research Council and Global Co-Chair of Asia Society. She is a Member of the Science of Cities Committee, National Research Foundation; a Member of the Board of Trustees of NUS; a Member of the Yale-NUS Governing Board and a Member of the Presidential Council for Minority Rights. In her diplomatic career, she was Singapore's Ambassador to the US and Singapore's Permanent Representative to the UN with concurrent accreditation as High Commissioner to Canada and Ambassador to Mexico.

ABOUT THE COVER ILLUSTRATOR

Esther Goh (esthergoh.co) is a Singapore-based illustrator and art director whose works span the areas of interactive design, branding and print. Her illustrations have been recognised and published internationally.

Lecture I
GRAND TRANSITIONS: OUR MULTILATERAL JOURNEY

LECTURE I

The Multilateral Moment

Let me start my first lecture by bringing you on a brief journey through time.

At the dawn of the second decade of the 21st century, United Nations (UN) Secretary-General António Guterres began his 2020 New Year address by describing "four horsemen" in our midst — looming threats that endanger 21st century progress and 21st century possibilities. He described them as global geostrategic tensions, existential climate crisis, deep and growing global mistrust, and the dark side of the digital world. In September 2020, at the opening of the General Assembly to commemorate the 75th Anniversary of the UN, he added a fifth horseman: the global COVID-19 pandemic.

Our world is more interconnected than ever with the convergence of the global and the local. The nature of interconnectedness and integration that defines our time means that the biggest economic and societal forces disrupting and transforming the world can either jeopardise our shared future or secure it, depending on our governance mindset, our choices and the way we act now, not just locally but globally.

As we imagine the future, there is much to learn by reflecting on our past. I invite you to cast your mind back to 75 years ago when the world made a pivot, a grand transition that transformed its future and has profoundly shaped our present. Our world had witnessed the unspeakable atrocities and devastation of World War II (WWII), when the dominant economic and military powers wielded ideology and violence to assert their self-interests. WWII is said to be the deadliest war in history, with an estimated 85 million death toll, including the millions who perished in the Holocaust. It is perhaps difficult for us to imagine what the world was like then, not even 100 years ago — severely wounded, fundamentally fragmented, deeply dehumanised. These lines by the great Russian poet, Anna Akhmatova, in her poem *Requiem* about the victims and survivors of Stalin's Great Purge, capture something of the living nightmare of war:

> *That was a time when only the dead*
> *could smile, delivered from their wars.*[1]

This global war came to an end in Asia, several months after it had ended in Europe, not through a peace accord but in the aftermath of the atomic bombings of the cities of Hiroshima and Nagasaki. Human history had never seen death and devastation of this scale. We were forced to confront what we, the human species, are capable of doing to each other and to our world. We were forced to ask ourselves existential, moral and political questions: What is the value of human life? How can we begin a new chapter after such terrible darkness? How can nations forge a new path of international understanding to salvage what remains of civilisation and attempt to restore our humanity? What are the shared principles that would form the foundations of our collective future?

---

[1] Anna Akhmatova, "Requiem," in *Poems of Akhmatova*, trans. Stanley Kunitz and Max Hayward (Boston: Houghton Mifflin, 1997), 99.

From the ash and rubble of WWII, world leaders of 50 nations came together to reimagine a dramatically different future, finding pathways to rebuild anew. In 1945, they found a path that offered the world the hope of peace. They came together in San Francisco to forge an inclusive rule-based multilateral world order for big and small nations coming out of colonialism based on the principles of the UN Charter. Their plan was nothing less than the restructuring of the world order based on mutual trust and cooperation guaranteed by the leadership of the United States (US), the major global power that emerged after the war. This was the multilateral moment that transformed our world, based on a recognition of the need for justice and respect for international law, promising to save succeeding generations from the scourge of war, from the propensity of the human species for self-destruction.

The UN Charter, in its preamble which begins with "We the Peoples", ensures fundamental human rights, the equal rights of men and women, of nations large and small, and promises every individual in every country an equal claim to dignity, respect and happiness, and in larger freedom, free from want and free from fear. They believed in the value of collective efforts and multilateral governance founded on the UN, to achieve social progress and better standards of life for individuals and nations. The UN became the global body with universal participation and unquestioned legitimacy to guide the world into new possibilities. This was the euphoric founding moment of the UN.

The world that my generation inherited was forged by these leaders, with the kind of long-term vision and values, solidarity and multilateral cooperation that brought giant leaps in our living standards. The UN Charter is an exceptional achievement of solidarity. For over the last seven decades, the practice of its international norms and the support given by UN institutions have largely delivered independence, peace, prosperity, justice, human rights, hope and support for billions of people.

For many others, however, these aspirations were never realised and are now receding in a dangerous era of uncertainty and anxiety. Despite our best efforts, too many people have remained marginalised and left behind, facing a bleak future if we do not act fast.

"Guardian of the Charter": Successes and Failures

The marking of the UN's 75th Anniversary in 2021 saw a process of deep reflection globally on how multilateralism can deliver effectively amidst the changing landscape of threats and opportunities. It prompted discussions on how well the UN has fulfilled its mission as "Guardian of the Charter" using its legitimacy, convening authority and normative power. It sought to identify the kind of innovations in multilateral governance that are needed to find solutions to 21st century challenges in a new era of uncertainty, anxiety and complexity.

As we learn from the UN's positive legacies as well as from its failures, we need to first understand the essential nature of the UN. By its very nature, the UN is a hierarchical intergovernmental organisation where governments with diverse powers and governance structures make decisions that affect the direction and functioning of the UN. At the same time, the UN has a strong history of mobilisation and partnership based on the values and moral authority of the UN Charter. It has opened new possibilities, created spaces and built alliances to create a more people-centred multilateralism that has brought about social change and accountability, especially with women and civil society. Its multilateral governance operates along four main pathways:

1) Peace and Security — the idea that we can create a system of collective security, built on negotiation and mediation, so as to avoid the use of force except in self-defence or as authorised by the UN Security Council.
2) Independence — the idea that people in all countries have the right to be politically independent and sovereign, based on the choices of their citizens.
3) Development — the idea that all countries must pursue economic and social policies that would improve the well-being and living standards of their population.

4) Human Rights — the idea that every individual in every country shares an equal claim not only to individual civil and political rights, but also a core of more collective economic and social rights.

The UN Charter and the four pathways consolidated the international consensus, formed the foundation of multilateral governance and showed how it should function globally and locally.

Let me illustrate the functioning of these multilateral governance pathways from the rooted reality of human experiences and the perspective of "We the Peoples", as governance is as much about practice as it is about norms and legal frameworks.

Peace and Security

The age of decolonisation and the workings of multilateral governance unfolded not in a climate of international stability and harmony, but in the ominous shadow of the Cold War and its battles for ideological hegemony. Since this lecture is held on 16 November, the UN International Day for Tolerance, let me recall an example of preventive diplomacy in the handling of the Cuban Missile Crisis in 1962, which almost led to a nuclear confrontation between the two big powers, the US and the Soviet Union.

The confrontation from the Cuban Missile Crisis is often considered the closest the Cold War came to escalating into a full-scale nuclear war, which would have destroyed much of humanity. The use of preventive diplomacy by then UN Secretary-General U Thant was critical. He was hands-on, on the ground and behind the scenes when the crisis loomed large. As a mediator for global security, he was trusted by all sides and worked diligently to resolve the most dangerous conflict of his time.

U Thant was the first non-European to take the helm of the UN at the height of decolonisation, when newly independent states joined the UN as equal members of the international community, dramatically shifting the balance of power within the UN and ushering in the greatest transformation of sovereign power in modern history. From 1945 to the end of U Thant's tenure as Secretary-General in 1971, the UN member states grew from a mere 51 to 132 (today there are 193). U Thant, himself from a newly independent nation, Burma, understood just how significant this political transformation was. He understood that the acceptance and tolerance of diversity and difference lay at the heart not only of democracy, but also of peace and security.

With wise foresight, U Thant realised the importance of protecting diversity in a decolonising world, freeing itself from the Age of Empire. For him, diversity was both a reality and a non-negotiable principle for the new international order. He knew that given the very deep historical roots of colonialism, imperialism and inequality, the values of equal rights and diversity cannot be taken for granted. They had to be actively protected and safeguarded for our common future. Not accepting diversity meant rejecting a multilateral world built on peaceful coexistence, and mutual respect for countries big and small, and for all people. The alternative was unthinkable, a direct attack on peace and the possibility of a shared future. He understood that leadership from the UN Secretary-General was required, one that was ready to defend the principles and values that lay the foundations for the very possibility of peaceful coexistence, to make the world safe for diversity. He often said, "As a Buddhist, I was trained to be tolerant of everything except intolerance."[2]

Sovereignty: Recognition of Nation States

The power of the UN's unquestioned legitimacy is perhaps best illustrated in its accreditation and recognition of nation states, big and small. In granting recognition and sovereignty, there is also the expectation that national constitutions are aligned with the values of the UN Charter and that nation states function as responsible "global citizens". Singapore is a prime example of this, being one of the smallest states in the world. Prime Minister Lee Hsien Loong, in 2015, writes in his foreword for the book *50 Years of Singapore and the United Nations*, edited by Tommy Koh et al.:

---
[2] U Thant, *View from the UN* (Newton Abbot: David Charles, 1978), 69.

> *Singapore became independent on 9 August 1965. One of the first things which the new republic did was to apply to join the United Nations. As our first Foreign Minister, Mr S. Rajaratnam, explained, we did this to obtain from the UN "an international endorsement of Singapore's sovereignty and integrity". On 21 September 1965, Singapore was admitted as the UN's 117th member state.*[3]

The symphony of voices from our leaders captures the critical importance of this moment for Singapore as it emerged as a new nation, a city-state integrated into the global community. In the preface of his 2015 book, Professor Tommy Koh, along with his co-editors, said:

> *The story begins in 1965 when Singapore was expelled from the Federation of Malaysia and became a sovereign and independent country. At the time of its birth, there were critics, both at home and abroad, who had cast doubts on the legitimacy of Singapore's independence. It was therefore an imperative for Singapore to seek admission to the UN.*[4]

S. Rajaratnam, then Foreign Minister of Singapore, spoke powerfully to the UN General Assembly on 21 September 1965, on the occasion of Singapore's admission to the UN:

> *My country will join with other nations in their efforts to realise the aims and objectives of the United Nations Charter. For us the essentials of the Charter are the preservation of peace through collective security, promotion of economic development through mutual aid and the safeguarding of the inalienable right of every country to establish forms of government in accordance with the wishes of its own people. … We support these ideals because we*

---

[3] Lee Hsien Loong, "Foreword," in *50 Years of Singapore and the United Nations*, ed. Tommy Koh, Li Lin Chang, and Joanna Koh (Singapore: World Scientific, 2015), v.

[4] Tommy Koh, Li Lin Chang, and Joanna Koh, "Preface," in *50 Years of Singapore and the United Nations*, ed. Tommy Koh, Li Lin Chang, and Joanna Koh (Singapore: World Scientific, 2015), ix–xii.

realise that the well-being, the security and integrity of my country can be assured only on the basis of these principles. ***It is practical self-interest and not vague idealism which makes it necessary for my country to give loyal support to these essential elements in the UN Charter.*** *World peace is a necessary condition for the political and economic survival of small countries, like Singapore. ... So it is natural that my country should adhere firmly to the policy of resolving differences between nations through peaceful negotiation; by non-violent means.*[5]

Indeed, there is a happy history and relationship between Singapore and the UN. Singapore has benefitted from its membership of the UN since its early years of independence when it was a fragile new nation and our future was uncertain. Singapore used its sovereignty to build the Singapore core; a nation based on multiracialism and meritocracy, and developed economic and social strategies to build new possibilities for its citizens. The UN institutions provided Singapore with many benefits, such as soft loans from the World Bank, technical assistance and expert advice from the United Nations Development Programme (UNDP), the United Nations Children's Fund (UNICEF) and the United Nations Industrial Development Organization (UNIDO). One of the UN experts, Albert Winsemius of the Netherlands, was subsequently appointed by the Singapore government as its economic adviser. At the same time, Singapore and Singaporeans have contributed to the work of the UN and to multilateral governance. More will be discussed in my next two lectures.

Development

When the UN was founded 76 years ago in 1945, close to a third of the world's population was under colonial rule. The decades that followed saw a process of decolonisation throughout the world, with newly independent

---

[5] NAS, "Statement of His Excellency S. Rajaratnam Foreign Minister of Singapore at the General Assembly on September 21 on the Occasion of Singapore's Admission to the United Nations," New York, September 21, 1965, https://www.nas.gov.sg/archivesonline/data/pdfdoc/PressR19650921.pdf.

countries joining the UN as member states. In this context, a key mission of multilateral governance was to help newly independent countries emerge economically and socially from the historical subjugation, discrimination and exploitation of colonialism. Multilateral institutions of the UN and its sister institutions, the International Monetary Fund (IMF) and the World Bank, were created to support sovereign states to generate economic growth to end poverty and economic exploitation. They were charged with three critical missions: promoting international monetary cooperation; supporting the expansion of industrialisation, trade and economic growth, and encouraging policies that would generate shared prosperity and social development.

However, having high aspirations is only the start. The harder part is supporting countries to change their direction and practice of development, especially at pivotal moments, to improve the human prospect and to raise the standards of life for the population at large, not just for the leaders and the elites of these new nations.

Many newly independent countries were caught between the exclusive approaches and binary opposition of the superpowers engaged in the Cold War. From the shaping of national identity, citizenship rights, the direction of development, the nature of governance and citizens' engagement, there were limits and consequences determined by the Cold War divide that cast its long shadow on societies still reeling from the legacy of colonial history. The opening of the Iron Curtain that divided Europe, symbolised by the fall of the Berlin Wall on 9 November 1989, marked the beginning of the end of the Cold War era. As countries of the former communist bloc began to integrate into the global market economy, globalisation became a common pathway for development. The UN could again wield the moral authority of its Charter to mobilise the collective power of nations to work together for renewed economic and social progress to shape a fairer globalising world. It was a turning point of great promise.

Yet, our globalised world requires an effective system of checks and balances to ensure that human development is prioritised, not simply political power and economic growth. In the years that followed the end of the Cold War, governments gathered to address how to shape a more inclusive and sustainable world order through an unprecedented series of UN world conferences, starting with the World Summit on Children (1990); the Earth Summit (1992); the World Conference on Human Rights (1993); the International Conference on Population and Development (1994); the World Summit for Social Development (1995); and the Fourth World Conference on Women (1995).

In addition, the UNDP published the first Human Development Report in 1990 by economist Mahbub ul Haq and Nobel Laureate Amartya Sen.[6] It provided an inspiring and theoretically grounded framework that focused on people and how development is more than just the quantity of growth based on gross national product (GNP). The IMF and World Bank started to go beyond their early structural adjustment approach and began to focus on poverty, growth and economic restructuring, as reflected in the World Bank's 1990 World Development Report.

The outcomes from the UN conferences and their five yearly reviews were consolidated into the Millennium Development Goals (MDGs) in 2000 and later into the 2030 Agenda for Sustainable Development in 2015. Together with the 2015 Paris Climate Agreement, the 2030 Agenda: Transforming Our World provides a very good framework for development using the synergetic holistic approach to emphasise the interconnections across sectors and policies in our economy, society and environment. It is a multidimensional, transformational and collaborative approach to bring together the 5Ps of people, planet, prosperity, peace and partnership, with human rights upfront. This reflects the values and principles of the UN Charter and the comprehensive nature of the 2030 Agenda on Sustainable Development leaving no one behind. The message is clear: to prevent warfare we need welfare, the well-being of people and planet globally and locally. In the words of former UN Secretary-General Ban Ki-Moon, "[The Paris

---

[6] UNDP, *Human Development Report 1990: Concept and Measurement of Human Development* (New York: Oxford University Press, 1990).

Agreement] is a health insurance policy for the planet. It is the most significant action in years to uphold our Charter mandate to 'save succeeding generations.'"[7]

What happens next comes down to choices. Political leaders and policymakers in every country and region have a range of choices to practice good governance to transform society and improve people's lives. Since our inception as a nation, our mindset, choices, foundations and partnerships have helped shape today's Singapore and, together with our region, create "Rising Asia".

Insights From Rising Asia
Good Governance Matters

Much of Asia enjoyed at least 60 years of stability, peace and prosperity due to the creation of the global order founded on the rules of multilateralism. During this period, Asia transformed itself as countries began to generate economic growth through developing their natural resources, human resources, capital investment and technological capacities, and searched for governance systems that would support these priorities. The region reduced more than half the population living in poverty. It created an expanding educated middle class. This is the crux of the Asian Miracle — the generation of rapid economic growth and the reduction of poverty in the shortest period of human history.

The Asian Miracle came about as many founding leaders sought to build "the developmental state", with strong public institutions to overturn historical vulnerabilities and to be in control of their own destiny. Singapore's founding Prime Minister Lee Kuan Yew strove for a new social contract between citizens and the nation to improve people's living standard by reducing poverty, creating intergenerational mobility and restructuring social and economic arrangements to achieve development ambitions. This

---

[7] Ban Ki-Moon, Opening Remarks at Press Encounter after Paris COP21 Conference, December 14, 2015, https://www.un.org/sg/en/content/sg/speeches/2015-12-14/opening-remarks-press-encounter.

was done through job-led growth; providing public housing, investing in human capital through health and education, building the productive sectors, the reallocation of the workforce from low productivity occupation to higher productivity jobs in manufacturing and services, and creating the building blocks for the knowledge economy. Today, "Rising Asia", despite very strong headwinds from the 2008 global financial crisis, still serves as a hub for international trade, investment, technology and innovation.

While many parts of Asia have made great progress investing in people-centred development and generating prosperity, far too many people are still left behind. Today, Asia accounts for about 30 per cent of the global population living in extreme poverty (less than US$1.90 a day), and 65 per cent of the world's rural youth.[8] The number of undernourished people in the Asia-Pacific region amounts to 350 million, which is about 51 per cent of the global total.[9] In addition, nearly a billion people work in poorly paid jobs with no social protection due to the large share of the informal sector in the region. All these figures are expected to worsen due to the COVID-19 pandemic. The Asian Miracle is an unfinished agenda and sustaining Asia's dynamism is made more difficult as we enter a new era of uncertainty and complexity.

Global-Local Impact on Governance

The global economy is changing beyond recognition, moving from the industrial age to the digital age, creating tensions in global interconnections. We now have a paradox. Although our world currently is more interconnected than ever, it is simultaneously drifting further apart. We are integrated through trade, through global financial flows, through our global

---

[8] ILO, "Asia-Pacific Employment and Social Outlook 2020," December 15, 2020, https://www.ilo.org/wcmsp5/groups/public/---asia/---ro-bangkok/---sro-bangkok/documents/publication/wcms_764084.pdf, 39–40; Asian Development Bank, "Key Indicators for Asia and the Pacific 2021," August 2021, https://www.adb.org/sites/default/files/publication/720461/ki2021.pdf, 9–10; International Fund for Agricultural Development, "2019 Rural Development Report: Creating Opportunities for Rural Youth," June 2019, https://www.ifad.org/documents/38714170/41133075/RDR_report.pdf/7282db66-2d67-b514-d004-5ec25d9729a0, 51–52.

[9] FAO, UNICEF, WFP and WHO, *Asia and the Pacific Regional Overview of Food Security and Nutrition 2020: Maternal and Child Diets at the Heart of Improving Nutrition* (Bangkok: FAO, 2021), 6–7.

production system of integrated supply chains and services. We are in the midst of an information and communications technology (ICT) revolution with 3 billion people connected to each other on the Internet. Yet, we are fragmenting in terms of power, decision-making and opportunities.

Today, we are at our richest but, at the same time, we are witnessing skewed and imbalanced wealth concentration, unparalleled in human history. The world's richest 1 per cent own almost half the world's wealth, according to the 2021 Credit Suisse's Global Wealth Report, highlighting the growing gap between the super-rich and everyone else.[10] Growing economic, social and political inequalities have become more intertwined than ever, posing a grievous threat to our social cohesion and to our dynamism. A high and increasing ratio of wealth to gross domestic product (GDP) also illustrates growing concerns regarding the concentration of political and business power linked to asset ownership in our countries, which many fear acts out of elite self-interest. IMF research tells us that less inequality is associated with more sustainable growth and poverty reduction. At the same time, excessive inequality is associated with marginalised people, damaged communities and eroded trust. It is no wonder that so many feel anger and frustration, with the sense that the rules of the game are unfair, unable to stamp out self-interest and corruption by powerful elites.

The backlash against globalisation accelerated with the 2008 global financial crisis which affected the real economy worldwide. The crisis increased household indebtedness and unemployment, and broke public trust and confidence, especially in the US and Europe. The financial crisis bailout for corporations that were "too big to fail", alongside the austerity for the middle class and the poor, discontent over inequality and concern over the climate crisis, fuelled a dissatisfaction with the status quo. When people start believing the economy no longer works for them, they start disconnecting from society. Excluded groups, women and youth mobilised locally and globally for change and many were inclined to disrupt the

---

[10] Credit Suisse, "Global Wealth Report 2021," June 2021, https://www.credit-suisse.com/about-us/en/reports-research/global-wealth-report.html.

established order that did not work for them. Pressures worldwide were created for greater transparency, stronger corporate governance and accountability in the financial and banking sectors, including from citizens' movements like Occupy Wall Street. In major Western capitals, attention began to focus on the concentration of wealth and power, corruption, the corporate capture of the state and questioning the value of global governance and its institutions. As the quality of governance became an issue of increasing concern in both developed and developing countries, human rights have come under pressure.

Human Rights

After two successive world wars and their genocides, our founders in the UN Charter reaffirmed their "faith in fundamental human rights, in the dignity and worth of the human person" and committed all member states to promote "universal respect for, and observance of, human rights and fundamental freedoms for all without distinction as to race, sex, language or religion."[11]

Today I will limit my discussion of human rights to economic and social rights, in the context of Asia's economic development. I will focus on the human rights responsibility of corporate entities given the power they exercise and critical accountability gaps in corporate governance that are associated with being a non-state actor.

Asia's phenomenal growth over the past few decades was driven by "Factory Asia". As the world's largest workshop, Asia surged ahead by providing cheap and abundant labour, formal and informal, to produce very rapidly, and at very low cost, much of the manufactured consumer goods that the world needed. With the unprecedented economic reform unleashed in China in late 1980s, production networks and supply chains were born. The Association of Southeast Asian Nations (ASEAN) benefited from the regional production networks, producing intermediate products

---

[11] UN, "Universal Declaration of Human Rights," December 1948, https://www.un.org/en/about-us/universal-declaration-of-human-rights.

cheaply for the world market. This model of growth created jobs and prosperity. But it was prosperity that was not shared. Inequality grew rapidly in Asia. Jobs were created, but in many sectors the right to work sacrificed rights at work, especially for young women and migrant workers, as factories competed in the race to the bottom on labour standards and human rights.

In this race, many factories ignored safety, health and labour standards, ignored how they disposed of their toxic waste, ignored human trafficking, ignored what they did to the environment and how they grabbed and acquired land from the communities. Our civil societies raised the alarm, many leaders were arrested and human rights defenders disappeared as state-people governance declined in some countries. Major wake up calls came with several human and environmental tragedies too big to ignore, and the urgency to move towards a new economic paradigm, responsible capitalism, as well as accountable business conduct and governance that recognises that respect for human rights creates value.

In Asia, yet another wake-up call for workers' rights came with the 24 April 2013 Rana Plaza incident in Bangladesh. The building, which housed five garment factories, collapsed, leaving at least 1,132 garment workers, mainly young women, buried alive and over 2,500 injured, many missing arms and legs. Workers without rights were ordered back to work to meet deadlines for 27 global brands, despite official knowledge that the eight-storey building was unsafe. Workers under threat had to turn around vast quantities of clothes very rapidly and cheaply for global markets. This tragedy shocked the world and came in the wake of a series of other disasters in the region from factory fires, mining collapse, floods and cyclones, to worker walk-outs and kidnappings of CEOs, to the haze created by the unsustainable cultivation and deforestation practices of palm oil companies.

Clearly, business as usual was no longer an option. It can no longer be siloed from other areas of international agenda setting and decision-making. It requires a rethinking of the interdependence between the economy, people and planet, a shift from the quantity of growth mindset to generate profit at any cost, to the quality growth for the well-being of people and planet.

A strong tripartite social contract anchored in human rights between corporations, government and workers, modelled on the practice of International Labour Organization (ILO), is the foundation for moving forward. Good corporate governance underpinned by the social contract will have profound consequences for people, shaping their life chances and the well-being of communities.

UN Standards for Responsible Business and Human Rights

Today, the adoption and implementation of international responsible business practices, which not only generates financial returns but also contributes to inclusive and sustainable development, while minimising negative impacts on environment and society, has gained increased attention from both governments and enterprises, besides civil society organisations. A series of UN conventions and agreements form the basis for international norms on human rights, labour and the environment. Most of the global corporate social responsibility (CSR) instruments either take these as their starting point or align their content with these. They include the UN Universal Declaration of Human Rights, the ILO Declaration on Fundamental Principles and Rights at Work, the UN Convention against Corruption, and environmental conventions including the Paris Climate Agreement.

Existing voluntary CSR instruments like the UN Global Compact and the UN Guiding Principles (UNGPs) for Business and Human Rights also provide a useful framework for corporate governance and businesses. The UN Global Compact, launched in July 2000, consists of 10 principles in the four areas of human rights, labour, the environment and anti-corruption. Many companies have now signed up to implement the 10 principles in their core operations and annually report on their progress.

The UNGPs for Business and Human Rights were endorsed by the UN Human Rights Council in June 2011. They comprise three pillars: (i) state duty to protect human rights, (ii) corporate responsibility to respect human rights and (iii) access to remedy for victims of business-related human rights abuse. These principles have been integrated into environment, social and governance (ESG), principles and business agendas.

Moving from Standards to Implementation

Asia is at a crossroads. It became "Factory Asia" when the region was a very different place: a battleground for both superpowers and local wars, and poverty devastated large parts of the region and people's lives. Today, Asia has become a powerhouse, the centre of gravity of the global economic recovery. Many parts of Asia, including ASEAN, have gone beyond "Sweatshop Asia" with an expanding middle class, towards a higher educated, richer and technologically advanced population. Singapore, in particular, having placed a high premium on quality education, healthcare, and jobs and skills training for the future, moved quickly into the high-skilled knowledge economy and established the Workplace Safety and Health Act in 2006 to replace the Factories Act of 1973.

It is time for Asia to differentiate good business from bad business, to rethink, to change our development script, to take another leap and to invest in ourselves — in our people, cities, rural communities, the safety of our food, the quality of our air, our land, our water and energy systems. We can start to shift from short-term self-interest to long-term collective interest at whatever stage of our development journey. While a section of business is at the core of the problem, business has to be an important part of the solution as we seek to create a sustainable future and shared prosperity for all.

To stimulate strong regional markets and increase aggregate demands, we must focus on expanding opportunities for decent productive work and providing fair and equitable ways for all people to earn a living. Our business sector, as the principal source of jobs, plays the central role in this endeavour. In short, the future of Asian business rests in helping to realise an equitable economic system that works for people and the planet, in being a critical player in a global system that is best suited to the economic and social needs of the 21st century world. This shift will help to rebuild solidarity and contribute to the stewardship of our global commons and global public goods.

Solidarity as Self-Interest

When we all face the same threat, cooperation and solidarity are the only solutions, within societies and between nations. However, solidarity is weakened by broken trust, and the mismatch between promises and the realities of people's daily lives. Although international cooperation is key to resolving global problems, solidarity is in short supply as multilateral governance struggles to handle the interlocking disruptions of the global pandemic, climate crisis, our cyber world and our conflicts. In our interconnected and turbulent world, the well-being of one is dependent on the well-being of others. How do we embrace and enact the principle of solidarity as a society and as a nation?

Singapore's Multilateral Journey: From "Practical Self-Interest" to Common Interest

Our island of Singapore is a small nation state, and yet we have become a force to reckon with in the region and the world. How has Singapore experienced multilateral governance and how can the country contribute to its strengthening?

Singapore from the very start of nationhood realised that as a small state, it survives better in a world governed by the rule of law and where there are international norms that respect the sovereignty of nations. Foreign Minister Rajaratnam called it "practical self-interest".[12] This is still the core of our multilateral engagement, as repeated by several leaders and diplomats over time.

---

[12] NAS, "Statement of His Excellency S. Rajaratnam Foreign Minister of Singapore at the General Assembly on September 21 on the Occasion of Singapore's Admission to the United Nations," New York, September 21, 1965, https://www.nas.gov.sg/archivesonline/data/pdfdoc/PressR19650921.pdf.

Small countries need the UN and other international institutions to protect our interests and we therefore have every interest in making sure that these institutions are effective.[13]

Former Foreign Minister George Yeo (2008)

As a small state, [Singapore has] an abiding interest in strengthening the rules-based framework through the adoption of treaties, norms and guidelines. More importantly, we have a greater interest in ensuring that any treaties or rules adopted are in line with Singapore's interests or, at the least, not inimical to Singapore's interests.[14]

Burhan Gafoor, Permanent Representative of Singapore to the United Nations (2015)

However, Singapore has also been strategic in the way it has used its size for coalition building to build strength in numbers. In 1992, Ambassador Chew Tai Soo promoted the idea of the Forum of Small States (FOSS) in the UN to provide a platform for small states (population 10 million and below) to share information and strategies. Initiated by Singapore, the FOSS allowed small states to work together on issues of mutual interest, lend a greater voice to views and concerns of small states, and raise their international profile. To quote Minister K. Shanmugam (2013):

Due to our small size, we are ultimately "price-takers".... However, we have found strength in numbers by being united in international fora such as the UN.... Working together has given us a bigger

---

[13] MFA, "Speech by Minister for Foreign Affairs George Yeo at the 63rd Session of the United Nations General Assembly," September 29, 2008, https://www.mfa.gov.sg/Newsroom/Press-Statements-Transcripts-and-Photos/2008/09/Speech-by-Minister-for-Foreign-Affairs-George-Yeo-at-the-63rd-Session-of-the-United-Nations-General.

[14] Burhan Gafoor, "Merits of Multilateralism," in *50 Years of Singapore and the United Nations*, ed. Tommy Koh, Li Lin Chang, and Joanna Koh (Singapore: World Scientific, 2015), 79.

and louder voice collectively, and helped us amplify our own perspectives on global issues.[15]

Singapore's strategy in multilateral governance has been largely underpinned by Singapore's sense of vulnerability and price-taker status despite its proactive self-conscious attempts to overcome such constraints. Its initiatives in global governance are driven by means-end logic: to utilise the most efficient means to deliver the outcomes to protect its national interests to create a more predictable rule-based order favourable to small state survival.

The UN has not only protected Singapore because it embodies and entrenches a rule-based international system, but also because it provides a platform for small countries to build a network of friends and enlarge their diplomatic and geopolitical space. It provides small countries an opportunity to play a constructive role globally and thereby increase their profile within the community of nations. Singapore, as a small country, clearly understands but often struggles to fully embrace "solidarity as self-interest". While that principle endures in our changing world, the rule-based multilateral system that gave rise to it has been weakened, unable to effectively respond to the five horsemen described by the UN Secretary-General. The acceptance of collective thought and action, the very essence of multilateral governance, has been largely ignored as powerful countries are also acting out of self-interest.

After a year of listening and conducting consultations globally, the UN Secretary-General put forward Our Common Agenda as we reach a dangerous crossroads in our multilateral journey.[16] According to the Secretary-General, we have a choice: take the road to breakdown or the road to breakthrough. This depends on the deepening of solidarity to deal

---

[15] MFA, "MFA Press Statement: Caribbean Community (CARICOM) High-Level Ministerial Exchange Visit in Singapore 15 to 19 July 2013," July 15, 2013, https://www.mfa.gov.sg/Newsroom/Press-Statements-Transcripts-and-Photos/2013/07/MFA-Press-Statement-Caribbean-Community-CARICOM-HighLevel-Ministerial-Exchange-Visit_20130715.

[16] UN, *Our Common Agenda — Report of the Secretary-General* (New York: United Nations, 2021).

with our global commons: our oceans and our air and our global public goods: global health, the global and digital economy, peace and security, and our healthy planet. Our Common Agenda put forward concrete mechanisms and actions for a breakthrough. For their successful implementation, we need the same burst of energy and solidarity at the birth of the UN, to revitalise multilateral governance to effectively mobilise shared solutions to regional and global challenges of the 21st century.

Multilateral governance works best with responsible corporate governance and when effective democratic governance is practised by member states of the UN. How can Singapore contribute meaningfully to a strengthened system of multilateral governance? Examples of how Singapore has done this and where we now need to do more for our own interest will be examined in my next lecture. Singapore's multilateral journey is not simply a matter of national interest, it is a recognition and affirmation of our common humanity in the community of nations.

Question-and-Answer Session
Moderated by Mr Ho Kwon Ping

Dr Noeleen Heyzer speaking with Mr Ho Kwon Ping at her Q&A session
Source: Jacky Ho for the Institute of Policy Studies

Mr Ho Kwon Ping: Noeleen, I must say I have to add my remarks to that of IPS Director Janadas Devan. He's known you for five years longer than me, I've known you for 45, but I think we both share the same views. Anyone who has known you knows your unrelenting optimism, fervent idealism and practical determination to follow on those ideals, as evidenced by your recent appointment at a time when most people would be enjoying retirement. You've taken on a truly Herculean task and we're really proud of you as our best representative to the UN.

However, this is going to be a bit more provocative. I think we could divide this into two broad areas. One is about the whole question of multilateral governance itself and the second will be a bit more about Singapore's contribution to greater multilateral governance.

Now, here's the provocative part I want to put to you. There's an undivided global view that the UN since WWII has done a truly massive job in uplifting the livelihoods of people all around the world in economic, social, human development, health development and so on. However, it has probably been a lot less successful in terms of resolving geopolitical conflicts. In fact, it seemed to me a bit ironic that you alluded to 1962 as a case study of how multilateral governance from the UN helped to diffuse a geopolitical problem. Ironic because 1962 was a long time ago. Where has the UN been since then? And people have become quite cynical, obviously, even more so today at a time of China–US tensions. People are even questioning the entire relevance of the UN.

One interesting question related to that is this: Do you think there's a specific historic event that marks the world starting to retreat from post-WWII to multilateralism?

Dr Noeleen Heyzer: Very provocative, thank you, Kwon Ping. My deepest thanks for moderating this session. There was a time of great promise after the fall of the Berlin Wall when all the UN member states came together through a series of UN World Conferences and tried to shape what globalisation could mean. Frankly, I thought there were several points where the weakening began. The first was what happened to the United States in 2001 with the attack of September 11. The terrorist attack on the World Trade Center shook the country very deeply. I was there at that time and I saw the shock on people's faces and it was very hard to get over. After that many things broke, including I would dare say, the human rights way of dealing with the "other".

Then, there was unfortunately what happened at the Security Council with the Iraq War, in which Secretary-General Kofi Annan said that the

US-led invasion was illegal. And now we know that there was not enough evidence for the invasion. All this disrupted the peace and security sector. But also, in the economic sector, there was the global financial crisis of 2008 that affected the real economy and real people's lives. What happened and how it was resolved exposed power dynamics and broke a lot of trust in major institutions and in globalisation. And I think that this distrust of the establishment to deliver the social and economic security that people needed was what led to the suspicion of the "other". Respect for diversity was also weakened. As a result, the principles that formed the foundation of global governance weakened.

Despite this, I think the UN has to be credited for preventing a third world war from happening. There are also many conflicts that we do not know how to end. And these conflicts have caused the displacement of people on a scale that we have never seen since WWII. Today, we have about 80 million people who are displaced. They are migrating, taking dangerous journeys overseas, facing all kinds of difficult situations, sacrificing their life savings to traffickers and smugglers, just to get a chance of a better life. Unfortunately, they are not welcome because there's fear and insecurity in both developed and developing countries.

Mr Ho: And that adds to the cynical view for people who say that the UN does a great job in global damage control. When developed countries close off their doors to economic or war refugees, the UN does a great job with damage control. But let's not go there anymore. There are many people like myself who greatly admire the UN on one aspect and are perhaps a bit more cynical on the political side.

Dr Heyzer: Just to come in, what I'm asking us to think about is *who* forms the UN. There are three UNs. Firstly, we have the UN Secretariat and the Secretary-General. There is also the UN of the member states. And lastly, the third UN that we hardly talk about: "We the Peoples" — the citizens, the private sector, the think tanks and whoever can contribute.

Mr Ho: That leads to the bigger question. Does the UN structure need reform?

Dr Heyzer: Exactly, this is why we need to talk about the new multilateralism.

Mr Ho: What is clearly faltering, and perhaps even failing, is the political structure of the UN as a member states' decision-making body that came out of WWII, which may not be applicable today. But [people should not] tar with a broad brush all the works of the Secretariat and the other organisations, and very importantly, the people who are benefiting from it.

Dr Heyzer: Exactly.

Mr Ho: So let's move to other areas closer to home. We have a two-pronged question on ASEAN. Firstly, as a regional organisation, could ASEAN play a greater role in global governance? Secondly, when we talk about multilateral governance, you are speaking mainly of the UN. But what about ASEAN's own dysfunctionalities and successes?

Dr Heyzer: Professor Tommy Koh and his team, in partnership with the rest of the ASEAN member states, created the ASEAN Charter. And the ASEAN Charter actually incorporated a lot of what was in the UN Charter. Also, if you look at it, the UN Charter has a whole article on regional organisations and the importance of regional organisations. So, the UN works very closely with ASEAN. In fact, when I was the Under-Secretary-General based in Bangkok at that time with the regional commission, we developed a comprehensive UN–ASEAN framework and partnership. This was absolutely critical because it actually assisted with the way we dealt with shared vulnerabilities. At that time, the biggest vulnerability was natural disasters. That's how the ASEAN Coordinating Centre for Humanitarian Assistance on Disaster Management (AHA) came in and the UN provided a lot of expertise and support in many of these disasters.

Also, the UN has tried to link in the ASEAN Community Vision 2025 to build a more integrated economy, with the UN's 2030 Sustainable Development Agenda. This is to ensure that the building up of the economic community is not just from the economic side but actually takes into account the three pillars of sustainable and inclusive development. A lot of the work that the UN actually does with ASEAN also goes in hand with ASEAN committees. For example, the ASEAN Commission on the Promotion and Protection of the Rights of Women and Children (ACWC), the work on the implementation of the Convention on the Elimination of All Forms of Discrimination Against Women (CEDAW) and so on, is incorporated.

Mr Ho: What can ASEAN do more?

Dr Heyzer: It's not easy. ASEAN itself consists of very different member states — at different stages of development, different interests and so on. So of course, when it comes to certain decision-making, it tends to be slow. And sometimes, even in crises, it's not seen to be fast enough.

There is a lot of frustration: "Why can't you all get your act together and just go on and do it?" But ASEAN treads very carefully. It's like taking two steps forward and three steps backwards. It's a kind of a dance. But increasingly, I think the UN is going to depend a lot more on regional organisations. We can think about ASEAN but we can also think of the African Union, for example. For many conflicts and wars, they are unfortunately so intertwined with regional dynamics, and thus regional institutions are needed.

Mr Ho: You're talking like a diplomat. What is the one change you would like to see within the ASEAN decision-making structure, knowing very well its realistic constraints?

Dr Heyzer: Here, I actually would take the cue and the example of our mutual friend who unfortunately has passed away, Dr Surin Pitsuwan. I really like the way he managed ASEAN as the 12th ASEAN Secretary-General. He did not wait for the consensus. Consensus-making very often would have to go down to the lowest common denominator. Dr Surin actually talked about the coalition of the willing. Those who don't want to agree, get out of the way. We who agree will move forward, we will take responsibility.

Mr Ho: So your suggestion is to have an absentee vote, not everybody has to vote.

Dr Heyzer: Yes, not everybody has to vote.

Mr Ho: Is that speaking as the next ASEAN Secretary-General?

Dr Heyzer: No, not me!

Mr Ho: Let's move to another very topical subject, COVID-19. What do you think has been the role — positive or negative — of multilateral governance in dealing with the whole outbreak and internationalising the control of it? In dealing with vaccine nationalism and its related issues, what are the lessons learnt? Further, COVID-19 has been even more devastating to poorer developing countries. What can the UN do to help mitigate this impact on the poorest countries of the world?

Dr Heyzer: I think one of the best things the UN did was to initiate COVID-19 Vaccines Global Access (COVAX). This was the facility that basically coordinated the distribution and manufacturing of the vaccine. There is going to be no economic or social recovery without vaccination. But of course, unfortunately, the richer countries buy up most of the vaccines and the poorer countries don't have much access, either to the manufacturing of the vaccine or to their distribution. And worse still if the country is in conflict. In fact, Singapore has played a very good role and became a member of COVAX very early on and contributed to the facility. It also contributed to the distribution of the vaccine to less developed countries. So there is cooperation that is going forward.

Even before COVAX, Secretary-General António Guterres went to the Security Council and wanted to get a Security Council resolution to bring the superpowers together for a coordinated and a powerful response — the way we did it with Ebola, where the US actually played a very strong role. However, the US administration did not go along with it, and there were geopolitical tensions with China and so on. So the Security Council resolution didn't quite happen and the Secretary-General eventually called for a global ceasefire to get the vaccines across to the conflict-affected countries. After months of negotiations, eventually something did happen. But that was very slow amidst all these tensions.

So, the World Health Organization (WHO); Gavi, the Vaccine Alliance; the Coalition for Epidemic Preparedness Innovations (CEPI) and many member states went forward and formed an alliance. It is not as coordinated as we could be, but it is happening. And increasingly, the Secretary-General actually did not just depend on the UN space, but called upon the Group of Twenty (G20) to take into account not just the immunisation programme but the manufacturing and the distribution of vaccines, as well as issues of intellectual property rights, to allow the poorer countries to manufacture their own vaccine and distribute it. This is so critical because at the end of the day, it is not enough for us to just distribute a few vaccines everywhere. We have to realise that there is not going to be an economic recovery anywhere if our weakest links are not attended to.

Mr Ho: I want to move on to Singapore. I think there's a very good conceptual question here that I'm sure we'd like to hear from you about. As we all know, the UN is not an enforcement agency. It has no coercive power; it has no military or police besides its peacekeeping forces. But it is a very powerful validator of social norms — what is acceptable and what is not acceptable — and to the extent that many of the parties that do not want these global social norms are in fact governments or rich corporations. The question here is, do you think civil society in every country plays a very important role, together with the UN, to create these norms? What is the role of civil society in working with multilateral agencies like the UN?

Dr Heyzer: It's huge. Although the UN is state-centric, it has the moral authority to give voice to the voiceless and to defend the defenceless. What it has done is the mobilisation of civil society. If you look at many UN conventions, civil society played a huge role. I myself was involved in the Fourth World Conference on Women, and I must say there were 30,000 women's groups organising from the ground up. And this was before the age of social media. This is because they wanted the norms and standards to come from reality, not something that was just formulated abstractly. It's also not just about norms and legal frameworks, but about practice and accountability. Because these norms can look very nice on paper, but when it comes to the practice, it is another thing.

Mr Ho: It must give you much more satisfaction, working with these groups rather than sitting in the General Assembly listening to politicians speak to empty halls.

Dr Heyzer: I wasn't going to go there, but I will.

Mr Ho: The answer is yes!

Dr Heyzer: I must say that within civil society, women are just absolutely wonderful as leaders, knowing how to use space and how to create alliances. Civil society knows how to form coalitions or alliances with member states that will support what you're doing. For example, our work on the Declaration on the Elimination of Violence Against Women was brought all the way up to the General Assembly. We didn't divide between civil society and the state, because there's no point if it is only civil society; the state has got to be accountable. So we worked with member states and got the declaration passed. For me, one of my greatest highlights when I was head of the UN Development Fund for Women (UNIFEM) was working with the Security Council.

Mr Ho: So you had to lobby in the corridors of power and then squat with villagers and discuss their problems.

Dr Heyzer: You have to go down to the floor, and your power is to be able to say to member states that you actually know what is happening on the ground and that these people on the ground know some of the solutions that you are looking for. It is important to bring both groups together. Because at the end of the day, for example with the Women, Peace and Security Agenda, if you are really interested in sustaining peace, you have to find the missing piece and knowledge that the people on the ground have.

Mr Ho: I'm going to be very provocative here. I think we all know the importance of the UN for Singapore as a small state. As S. Rajaratnam and other Ministers have said, we need the UN. That is not a point we have to prove at all. Neither does one have to prove that we as a small state have to work within the UN to be as effective as possible.

The provocative question is this: Singapore has said to punch above its weight, and we do. But we've always been very polite in not wanting to offend anybody. We all saw Barbadian Prime Minister Mia Amor Mottley scolding everyone at the UN. You cannot imagine a Singapore minister doing that, because we don't want to assert ourselves. And that has been our philosophy from the very beginning — we are a very small country. Now, what other ways can Singapore do more to recognise solidarity as self-interest, beyond respecting the UN and quietly trying to buttress the UN? Should Singapore play a more assertive leadership role?

Dr Heyzer: Well, I actually have two points to make. For one, besides the FOSS, Singapore also developed, under former Foreign Minister George Yeo, the Global Governance Group (3G). This was created to influence decision-making in the G20, and they have done that. But again this stems from self-interest, to make sure that the interests of the small states are attended to. This tends to be our default mode of operation, always putting our self-interest first. But I think in the future, there is an opportunity for Singapore to be in the lead, and I think Singapore will dare to do it because we have the capacity now; we want to be a digital hub for the region and even for the world. But now, one of the biggest things that we have to deal with that has not been spoken of much is that we have to ensure cyber security in the cyber world. Can Singapore shout and scream and try to get norms and standards that make sense? Increasingly, what we see in the real world can affect the cyber world, and even wars will be fought in cyberspace. So I think that Singapore, using our own voice but mobilising the voices of the small island states and the 3G, can shout a little bit more.

Mr Ho: So in the pursuit of enlightened self-interest, Singapore can push a bit harder.

Dr Heyzer: And to do that in the context of solidarity.

Mr Ho: To add on, we're a rich country. The resources of investment that we have, we can play with. We have a sovereign wealth fund and Temasek. If we combine all that and lead the way for developed countries in terms of climate finance, climate investment, and so on, we could probably move the needle considerably.

Dr Heyzer: Absolutely.

Mr Ho: Because right now that needle is moved by private equity funds, which as we all know has a lot of greenwashing.

Dr Heyzer: Yes. And also, while we can be an important financial centre, we need to have the right standards. Sometimes it is good for publicity, but we need to make it real.

Mr Ho: To end, I think I can say on behalf of everyone here that it's been an absolute delight to interact with you on your first lecture. I think all of us who know you believe that it's not only your intellectual rigour that's so admirable. It's particularly the fact that, as you've said to me many times, "What's the point of being an armchair critic? What's the point of being an armchair commentator? If you have the power, you have the resources, you have the will and the energy and the realistic idealism, go and do it!" And you are going to do it soon in a not-easy job. All of us wish you well and I think all of us agree there could not be any better person at all.

Dr Heyzer: Thank you, Kwon Ping.

Lecture II
GREAT DISRUPTIONS: THE STRUGGLE FOR OUR NORMATIVE FUTURE

LECTURE II

Our world has entered a new era of uncertainty, anxiety and complexity, overlaid by four great disruptions that have burst open historical fault lines, creating great fractures in their wake: the COVID-19 global pandemic revealing deep socio-economic divides; the climate crisis deepening intergenerational divides; the cyber world with its digital divide; and conflict with its peace and security divide. The handling of these disruptions combined with our shared vulnerability will be one of the greatest tests of our generation. The challenges we face in our interconnected but divided world are unprecedented. The United Nations (UN) Secretary-General António Guterres warns:

> We are at an inflection point in history. In our biggest shared test since World War II (WWII) humanity faces a stark and urgent choice: a breakdown or a breakthrough.[1]

The Secretary-General's warning is a wake-up call. In a scenario of breakdown and perpetual crisis, there will be deadly pandemics, the

---
[1] UN, *Our Common Agenda — Report of the Secretary-General* (New York: United Nations, 2021), 3.

planet will not be able to support life and there will be destabilising inequalities.

But if we have a scenario of breakthrough, we will have sustainable recovery, healthy people and planet, trust and social protection. The solutions that we seek will not be found country by country. The crises we face are global and resolving them depends on the effectiveness of multilateral governance. The scenario of breakdown with perpetual crisis is a clear possibility; but so too is the scenario of breakthrough with the prospect of an inclusive, sustainable and resilient future.

Just as the founders of the UN came together determined to save succeeding generations from the scourge of war, the purpose of multilateral governance in the 21st century is to come together to save succeeding generations from major existential risks to our future. While the fundamental purpose and principles of the United Nations endure, the world has changed, creating new needs that call for new normative frameworks and arrangements to address interlocking disruptions that are endangering the very safety and sustainability of human life: pandemics, the climate emergency, the dark side of the cyber world and armed conflict. In this lecture, I will discuss the four great disruptions and the struggle for new norms and practices in multilateral governance as we rethink sustainable recovery for equality, inclusion, sustainability and resilience in the post-COVID-19 world. In the process, I will consider how Singapore fares amidst these struggles, and if Singapore of today can be a key thought leader for change in the multilateral world.

Four Great Disruptions

Disruptions bring about radical change that transforms our lives and our world. They can either be a doorway to new possibilities or a force of destruction. It is up to us how we meet the challenge of these disruptions, and we do not have the luxury of time. The choices we make now, individually and collectively, will determine the fate of generations to come.

A great disruptor that links today with tomorrow, and this generation with the next, is climate change. It is one of the defining challenges of our time and its adverse impacts undermine the ability of all countries to sustain their development and provide human security. Climate change is already transforming ecological systems, changing weather patterns, impacting agricultural production, food and water security. From heat waves and flooding in Europe, to dust storms and air pollution in the major cities of Asia, to droughts in Africa, to conflicts over access to clean water and land use, to melting glaciers and rising sea levels, the effects of climate change are being felt all over the world, affecting the health, well-being and future of people and the planet.

Another very significant disruption of our time is the digital revolution. The rise of smart machines, artificial intelligence (AI) and robotics will have dramatic implications for jobs and the way we work and live. These new technologies hold great potential and will open up a whole new world for us, our children and generations to come. At the same time, however, these very technologies can also increase risk and accelerate inequality. Entire sectors of the labour market are disappearing. And although new opportunities are emerging, the jobs created are not the same. Our children may need to have more than one job and more than one career, engage in lifelong learning and keep gaining new skills over the course of their lifetime. Despite enormous benefits, new technologies are also being abused to commit crimes, incite hate, spread falsehoods, exploit and invade privacy. The pandemic has also demonstrated that digital solutions must be supported by strong cybersecurity frameworks to prevent cyberattacks on hospitals, medical research facilities and other essential infrastructure.

Amidst increasing vulnerability and challenges of sustainability, we also see trends of new political upheavals, while protracted conflicts that have lasted for decades remain without solutions in sight. Today, over 84 million people, or one in every 95 people, endure forced displacement due to persecution, conflict, ethnic cleansing and mass atrocities, combined with the inability of the international community to work together to effectively stop wars, protect civilians, and build and preserve peace. This massive forced displacement crisis has affected the national politics of developed countries. Amid heightened vulnerability and feelings of insecurity, we have witnessed a rise in the securitisation of national borders, with severe impacts on migrants and refugees, who are increasingly perceived as threats to national security. We are faced with new threats from the rise of violent extremism, from ethnonationalism, from the spread of hate speech helping to fuel xenophobia and from the weakening of norms and institutions that promote tolerance and justice. Protectionism, divisive politics, racism and narrow self-interest threaten to weaken the multilateral order and collective global interest.

The COVID-19 pandemic is a disruption like no other. Its economic, social and health impacts are unprecedented since WWII, and have magnified inequality, insecurity and humanitarian challenges worldwide. The impacts are playing out along the fault lines of inequalities — of wealth, decent jobs, access to resources, social protection and ability to influence decision-making. The most vulnerable people are the bottom 40 per cent. The World Bank reports that poverty has increased as a result of COVID-19, with 97 million more in poverty as a result of the pandemic.[2] The worst affected are daily wage workers, casual workers, informal sector workers and caregivers. For most of them, working from home means being out of a job. Livelihood losses have led to food insecurity, hunger, evictions and homelessness for people with no savings and social support. Our bottom billion have no access to social protection and affordable healthcare. Migrants have lost employment and remittances have declined by US$100 billion, leading to further misery.

The crisis has taken a disproportionate toll on women and girls. Women make up the majority of caregivers and healthcare workers. We know that many women and girls face greater risks of violence as we impose at-home

---

[2] Daniel Gerszon Mahler, et al., "Updated Estimates of the Impact of COVID-19 on Global Poverty: Turning the Corner on the Pandemic in 2021?" *World Bank Blogs*, June 24, 2021, https://blogs.worldbank.org/opendata/updated-estimates-impact-covid-19-global-poverty-turning-corner-pandemic-2021?cid=SHR_BlogSiteShare_EN_EXT.

isolation. We know that many women are bearing the brunt of the pandemic's social and economic impacts as they are concentrated in the hardest-hit sectors, the most vulnerable jobs and in informal employment with the least social protection. Girls have dropped out of school and child marriage has risen. In fact, the UN estimated that 23.8 million additional children may drop out or not have access to school due to the pandemic alone.[3]

The pandemic has also not stopped conflicts and displacement, with disastrous consequences for refugees, displaced people and undocumented migrants, making it dangerous or even impossible for many to live with mass raids, arrests and detentions. The illicit economy of human trafficking and smuggling are on the rise as people prefer to die trying. Addressing this inequality and social exclusion challenge is at the very core of sustainable recovery. By failing to protect the health and safety of our most vulnerable, we put our entire society at risk.

In our age of great disruptions, we need to pause and ask ourselves: are we heading towards a utopia of dreams and ideals, or the waking nightmare of a dystopia? If our material and technological progress is not rooted in a foundation of ethics and compassion, we will end up as slaves to our most advanced inventions. In his short story, "The Machine Stops", E. M. Forster presented a dystopian vision of civilisation in crisis:

> *But Humanity, in its desire for comfort, had over-reached itself. It had exploited the riches of nature too far. Quietly and complacently, it was sinking into decadence, and progress had come to mean the progress of the Machine.*[4]

How do we ensure that "progress" and "development" empower humanity and safeguard our natural world? What are the principles of global governance that can contribute to a sustainable and resilient future?

---

[3] UNESCO, "UN Secretary-General Warns of Education Catastrophe, Pointing to UNESCO Estimate of 24 Million Learners at Risk of Dropping Out," August 4, 2020, https://en.unesco.org/news/secretary-general-warns-education-catastrophe-pointing-unesco-estimate-24-million-learners-risk.

[4] E. M. Forster, "The Machine Stops," in *The Eternal Moment and Other Stories* (United States: Harcourt Brace & Company, 1970), 29–30.

Rethinking Sustainable Recovery in the COVID-19 World

What COVID-19 has shown is that eventually the weakest links will give way and infect other parts of society, and that the whole will suffer. We can't quarantine the problems of the forgotten and vulnerable in our societies. Sooner or later, they become everyone's problem. Only an inclusive global public health and socio-economic response will help suppress the virus, restart our economies and recover sustainably. This requires a three-pronged approach:

> i) A large-scale, coordinated and comprehensive health response. Universal access to health must be a critical global public good as controlling the pandemic is the main prerequisite for global recovery. We need COVID-19 vaccines that are affordable and universally accessible for everyone, everywhere.
>
> ii) Protect current core capacities to safeguard lives and livelihoods and address the devastating social and economic dimensions of the crisis, with a focus on expanding economic and social support to the most vulnerable, keeping households afloat, businesses solvent, supply chains functioning and institutions delivering services and social protection.
>
> iii) A recovery process that builds back better, leading to more inclusive, resilient and sustainable economies and societies as well as an international system that can protect our global commons and deliver on global public goods. Recovery is an opportunity to address the climate crisis, inequality, gaps in our social protection systems, the shift from quantity of growth to quality of life, global health security, placing the well-being of every person at the core.

Four priorities with new normative frameworks and action on existing agreements are needed to deliver and protect global public goods as we build back better:

> 1) **Tackling inequality to revive economies and livelihoods:** As COVID-19 unfolds as a global pandemic of unprecedented reach,

one thing is clear — COVID-19 has exacerbated inequalities. Not only are low-income and marginalised populations more exposed to risks, but the pandemic is also likely to entrench inequalities within and between countries. To recover from COVID-19 and prepare for future global pandemics in a fragmented world, we need to ask some hard questions: Are the institutions of 21st century capitalism equipped to protect the vulnerable, promote global public interest and prioritise global health security over commercial profits? What are the norms and values, public policies, civil society action and discourses we need — locally, nationally and globally — to combat inequalities that have made us so vulnerable in the first place? How can we promote a more inclusive and sustainable pandemic recovery?

2) **Bridging the digital divide:** We need to ensure people are not left behind in an increasingly digital world, where jobs and services are increasingly based on digital literacy and access. Affordable internet access and literacy are public goods that require investments to accelerate inclusive digital transformation, to promote e-commerce for small business, e-governments and e-services, digital connectivity, and information and communication technologies (ICT) in education. However, technological advances are moving faster than our ability to respond to — or even comprehend — them. We are not prepared for the profound impact of the digital world on the labour market and the very structure of society. Besides skills training to enter this world, people need to understand the dark side of the cyber world and develop new norms for cybersecurity.

3) **Greening the economy:** We must embed long-term sustainability as a core element in our global COVID-19 recovery. Striving to achieve the goal of net zero carbon emissions by 2050 is imperative to reduce greenhouse gas emissions, keep the worst impacts of climate change at bay and protect the ecosystem of our planet. We already have multilateral frameworks to strengthen international cooperation to ensure a sustainable future for all our people and for

our planet. The Paris Climate Agreement and Agenda 2030 make up a plan of action, the roadmap, for people, planet and prosperity. Their urgent implementation will be a decisive turning point in the global quest for a safer, more sustainable and prosperous future.

4) **Upholding human rights and good governance:** These are central to a rule-based multilateral governance, one that is able to deliver peace and security and address drivers of conflict. There has been an overall breakdown in trust in major institutions worldwide due to failures to deliver public goods that people need most, to be fair and inclusive, to tackle corruption, to provide reliable information and to make a difference in people's lives. Therefore, to build back better from the pandemic, we need to include respecting fundamental human rights and addressing longstanding concerns in relation to democratic space, justice and the rule of law. People are struggling to be heard and to participate in the decisions that affect them. Political leaders, institutions and influential actors need to identify gaps in state–people and business–community governance relations to promote greater inclusion, participation, trust and solidarity.

Normative Struggles for Our Future

COVID-19 has not only deepened vulnerabilities everywhere but has also brought new urgency to the choices before us. Even before the pandemic, we were witnessing a wave of protests, especially among youths across the world. While each situation is unique, they share common features. There was already a growing deficit of trust between people, especially the young, and political institutions and leaders. COVID-19 threw these concerns into even sharper focus. The young saw their future compromised as they compared their realities to lives of the powerful, many of whom increased their wealth during the pandemic. Severe austerity measures to deal with the global financial and debt crises, and now the pandemic, created deep social wounds: joblessness, lost opportunities, a sense of deprivation and insecurity especially among youth, marginalised communities, the loss of trust in established elites and institutions, and the desire to overthrow them.

People need agency and voice in crises and, more than ever, governments need to be open, responsive and accountable to the people they are seeking to protect. People want a greater say in decisions about their lives, greater opportunities and shared prosperity. They are calling for social and economic systems that work for everybody. They want gender and racial equality, their human dignity and human rights respected. Otherwise, the pandemic provides the perfect breeding ground for conspiracy theories, and space for ideologues and extremists to energise divisions and political support by demonising "the other", to manipulate narratives and advance their own normative frameworks and agendas, undermining the ability of multilateral governance to deal with global challenges and interlocking disruptions.

Multilateral governance has already become more difficult against the backdrop of a heightened sense of insecurity and unfairness, leading to a rise in populism, nationalist agendas and conspiracy theories, including in powerful states like the United States (US), the guarantor of the global rule-based order. As long as there is a disconnect between local people and the institutions that serve them, if people are no longer confident that the global rule-based system is working for them, there will be a deep crisis of trust, a loss of shared understanding and belief in the integrity of scientific information that guides global decision-making. The UN Secretary-General has warned that this "infodemic" affecting our world and the "war on science" must end by defending a common, empirically backed consensus around facts, science and knowledge on how we share our societies and this fragile planet.[5]

Unfortunately, trust in multilateral governance has also been weakened by a global economic system that, despite significant country variations,

---

[5] United Nations, "António Guterres: This is a Time for Science and Solidarity," April 14, 2020, https://www.un.org/en/un-coronavirus-communications-team/time-science-and-solidarity.

displays some critical features everywhere. It devalues women's work and provision of care and destroys the natural environment. It has led to an extreme concentration of wealth and power among the few while causing a deep sense of insecurity and desperation among the many, including the hollowing out of the middle class and income stagnation among workers in powerful economies. This, in turn, has further fuelled a range of unsettling political dynamics, including widespread disenchantment with mainstream politics, hostility towards elites and rising ethno-nationalism, often fuelled by ideas of a return to an imagined, greater past founded on a different normative framework, including on women's role and gender equality.

But going back is not the answer. Instead, we need to raise the bar for economic, social, environmental and gender justice to prevent a health crisis from turning into a human tragedy. There is an urgent need to rebuild trust and to value what matters to people and the planet. We need to put the inclusion, protection and participation of the excluded at the heart of a renewed global social contract, like the consensus that was forged at the birth of the UN. This requires a transformative framework of norms and practices best suited to the economic and social needs of the 21st century, which invests in the nexus of sustainable development, human security and peace. It requires widespread constructive engagement and action on what it means to place inclusion, sustainability, gender equality and social justice at the centre of our COVID-19 response, and that of the interlocking disruptions of our time. This is the normative struggle for our future as we respond to the pandemic and heal our divided world. If we fail, Dr Henry Kissinger, in his book *World Order*, warned that we might face "a period in which forces beyond the restraints of any order determine the future".[6]

---

[6] Henry Kissinger, "Introduction," in *World Order: Reflections on the Character of Nations and the Course of History* (London: Allen Lane/Penguin, 2014), 2.

Seizing the Opportunity for Change

As no single nation or government, however powerful, can address the great disruptions of our times on its own, there is rising interest to reinvigorate our capacity for international cooperation and collective action. The hard work of international cooperation must continue, moving past rising nationalism in domestic politics, weak governance practices at the national and corporate level, geopolitical rivalry and unilateral action of big powers that have weakened multilateral governance.

I will use three examples that have seized opportunities to rebuild trust in the system for the well-being of people and our planet:

i) Specific coalitions of member states have emerged and formed constructive engagements to develop constructive multilateral solutions to transnational problems. I will use the example of the coalition for "a people's vaccine", or vaccine multilateralism. I will demonstrate, using the example of the 30 country-strong Global Governance Group (3G), how medium and small countries can serve as effective champions of the international rule-based order.

ii) Multi-stakeholder alliances that emerge to develop practical responses to pressing problems like climate change. Generally, the multilateralism discussion is very state focused, but orienting it around urgent problems and seeking solutions at a time of geopolitical divisions requires opening the circle. This is most evident in actions around climate change, where cities, subnational governments, the private sector and youths are often in the lead. Gaining a better understanding of where and when non-state actors can make positive contributions is an important task ahead.

iii) The focus on women as game changers in global governance, using the principles of the international rule-based order to set new norms and legal frameworks of human security, human rights and human development. The story of multilateral governance is not just about its legal history but, importantly, its social history. Power functions not just through hierarchy and authority, or purely through laws and institutions, but also through networks and social movements, new forms of global cooperation rooted in community organising and strengthened by transnational solidarity. In the process, they shape a different form of multilateralism, going beyond inter-state cooperation and towards prioritising human well-being from the ground up.

Vaccine Multilateralism and Singapore

Right from its inception, the pandemic has been marred by a lack of international cooperation. The pandemic has been addressed through uncoordinated and generally isolated national responses. It has revealed the weakness of multilateral governance as rich countries follow nationalistic agendas, and multilateral institutions and norms have been found waning. However, the pandemic has also made it very clear that multilateralism, not nationalism, is the answer for recovery and to build back better. The pandemic offers a window of opportunity to help advance multilateral innovation such as giving a stronger voice and a mechanism to small and medium countries to engage in global health governance.

From the very start of the pandemic, UN Secretary-General Guterres has championed "a people's vaccine" and "vaccine equity". In fact, World Health Organization (WHO) Director-General Dr Tedros Adhanom Ghebreyesus has warned the world against "vaccine apartheid", and is, today, asking for a "pandemic treaty" with the discovery of a new variant, Omicron.[7]

The multilateral COVAX facility was established in April 2020 by the WHO, the United Nations International Children's Emergency Fund (UNICEF),

---

[7] Reuters, "World Has Entered Stage of 'Vaccine Apartheid' — WHO head," May 17, 2021, https://www.reuters.com/business/healthcare-pharmaceuticals/world-has-entered-stage-vaccine-apartheid-who-head-2021-05-17.

Gavi, the Vaccine Alliance and the Coalition for Epidemic Preparedness Innovations (CEPI) to organise the collective procurement of vaccines on behalf of more than 100 countries. Singapore was an early supporter of the COVAX Facility and was among the first countries to join. It is the only global initiative that is working with governments and manufacturers to ensure COVID-19 vaccines are available worldwide to both higher-income and lower-income countries.

Singapore recognises the importance of a coordinated multilateral response to overcome the impact of the pandemic. The term "vaccine multilateralism" was coined by Prime Minister (PM) Lee Hsien Loong at the Global Vaccine Summit 2020 to build back frameworks of international cooperation to adequately meet the COVID-19 challenge. To quote him:

> *Discovering, producing and distributing a safe and effective vaccine is vital to get life back to normal despite COVID-19. I hope that this summit will help focus our minds and resources, and forge partnerships to promote "vaccine multilateralism".*[8]

Singapore committed a US$5 million contribution to support 92 low- and lower-middle income countries' access to the COVAX Facility. In July 2021, at the Asia-Pacific Economic Cooperation (APEC) Informal Leaders' Retreat, PM Lee stressed:

> *Countries whose vaccination programmes are ahead should make their excess vaccine supplies available to others. Thus, Singapore intends to donate our vaccines under the COVAX initiative to other countries.*[9]

As Chair of the Forum of Small States (FOSS), Singapore has also been invited to be a member of the Access to COVID-19 Tools (ACT) Accelerator's

---

[8] PMO, "PM Lee Hsien Loong's Video Message at the Global Vaccine Summit," June 5, 2020, https://www.pmo.gov.sg/Newsroom/PM-Lee-Hsien-Loong-Global-Vaccine-Summit.

[9] PMO, "Intervention by PM Lee Hsien Loong at the APEC Informal Leaders' Retreat," July 16, 2021, https://www.pmo.gov.sg/Newsroom/PM-Lee-intervention-APEC-Informal-Leaders-Retreat-July-2021.

Facilitation Council, allowing Singapore to ensure that the perspectives of small states are considered in discussions about access. With significant advances in research and development by scientists, academia, the private sector and government, the ACT Accelerator has secured a way to end the acute phase of the pandemic by deploying the tests, treatments and vaccines the world needs.

In February 2021, the UN Secretary-General addressed the Security Council to propose the creation of an emergency task force by the Group of Twenty (G20) countries to prepare and help implement a global immunisation plan:

> *The roll out of COVID-19 vaccines is generating hope.... At this critical moment, vaccine equity is the biggest moral test before the global community.*[10]

He noted that progress on vaccination has been very unfair globally, with just 10 countries having administered 75 per cent of all vaccines when 130 countries have not yet received a single dose. He stressed that the G20 is well placed to prepare such a plan and coordinate its implementation, bringing together all with the required power, scientific expertise and financial capacities, as well as the WHO and international financial institutions.

The importance of vaccine multilateralism and COVAX has also been stressed and agreed upon by the 3G, initiated by Singapore to channel the views of small and medium economies more effectively to the G20.

In October 2021, PM Lee was invited to the G20 Summit in Rome with its agenda "People, Planet, Prosperity", which focused on a sustainable and inclusive recovery from COVID-19 and a commitment to protect our climate. He reinforced the UN Secretary-General's call

---

[10] United Nations, "Secretary-General Calls Vaccine Equity Biggest Moral Test for Global Community, as Security Council Considers Equitable Availability of Doses," February 17, 2021, https://www.un.org/press/en/2021/sc14438.doc.htm.

to build collective resilience through faster manufacturing and deployment of vaccines worldwide, and supported the G20's proposed reforms to improve global health governance and financing amid the pandemic. He shared how Singapore has used its logistics capability, airport and ultra-cold chain facilities to become a distribution hub for vaccines. This is a good example of how 3G, a coalition of 30 member states, has emerged to forge constructive engagement to push for change. Singapore, as a leading member of the 3G, has been able to champion the voice of small countries calling for vaccine equality to close gaps in global health security.[11]

Multi-Stakeholder Alliances for Climate Action

Even amidst the COVID-19 pandemic, the climate crisis remains the existential challenge of our time. Its adverse impacts will stall development, affect food security, fuel intense storms, rising seas and displacement, transform ecosystems, and threaten public health and human security. All the leaders at the recent 2021 United Nations Climate Change Conference (COP26) have warned that we are already at the tipping point. The pace and scale of what we need to do over the next three decades to reach the goal of net zero carbon emissions by 2050, to stabilise the global temperature rise at 1.5 degrees Celsius above pre-industrial levels and to prevent climate disaster, is huge. According to our best scientists, climate change with its consequences is a tragedy in the making but it is still not too late if we take immediate action. In the words of world-renowned scientist Stephen Hawking, "Climate change is one of the great dangers we face, and it's one we can prevent if we act now."[12]

Important reforms and concrete actions are needed to help with the economic and social transition to make substantial progress towards the goal of net zero carbon: greening our infrastructure, food production,

---

[11] PMO, "Intervention by PM Lee Hsien Loong on 'Global Economy and Global Health' at the G20 Rome Summit," October 30, 2021, https://www.pmo.gov.sg/Newsroom/Intervention-by-PM-Lee-Hsien-Loong-on-Global-Economy-and-Global-Health-at-the-G20-Rome-Summit.

[12] Pallab Ghosh, "Hawking Says Trump's Climate Stance Could Damage Earth," July 2, 2017, https://www.bbc.com/news/science-environment-40461726.

housing and transport systems; setting ambitious targets for fuel efficiency and clean energy transition; investing in green technology and jobs training, innovative solutions and green business opportunities for all communities, leaving no one behind; respecting climate science and embracing evidence-based decision-making; shifting production and consumption patterns; respecting our forests and oceans.

While governments remain essential in multilateral governance, the complex range of public policy and global cooperation challenges to address the climate emergency can only be solved through effective multi-stakeholder alliances that bridge state and non-state actors, as well as the global and local. Coalitions of like-minded actors coalescing around a common goal are essential for urgent collective action towards sustainable development. This approach involves gathering a wide variety of interested parties — governments, civil society, the private sector, philanthropy and international organisations — to lead specific initiatives. To date, 73 parties to the UN Framework Convention on Climate Change (UNFCCC), almost 400 cities, 768 businesses and 16 investors are working to achieve net zero carbon emissions by 2050.[13]

However, the UN Intergovernmental Panel on Climate Change (IPCC) report, released in August 2021 and prepared by 234 scientists from 66 countries, warns that time is running out as global warming of 2 degrees Celsius will be exceeded during the 21st century.[14] Unless rapid and deep reductions in carbon dioxide and other greenhouse gas emissions occur in the coming decades, achieving the goals of the 2015 Paris Agreement will be beyond reach. UN Secretary-General Guterres said that the IPCC report was nothing less than "code red for humanity".[15] He added that ahead of the COP26 climate conference in Glasgow in November, all

---

[13] SDG Knowledge Hub, International Institute for Sustainable Development, "73 Countries Commit to Net Zero CO2 Emissions by 2050," December 17, 2019, https://sdg.iisd.org/news/73-countries-commit-to-net-zero-co2-emissions-by-2050.

[14] IPCC, "Climate Change Widespread, Rapid, and Intensifying," August 9, 2021, https://www.ipcc.ch/2021/08/09/ar6-wg1-20210809-pr.

[15] United Nations, "IPCC Report: 'Code Red' for Human Driven Global Heating, Warns UN Chief," August 9, 2021, https://news.un.org/en/story/2021/08/1097362.

nations — especially advanced G20 economies — need to join the net zero emissions coalition, and reinforce their promise on slowing down and reversing global heating, with "credible, concrete, and enhanced Nationally Determined Contributions (NDCs)". In addition, he added:

> *I am asking corporate leaders to support a minimum international carbon price and align their portfolios with the Paris Agreement. The public and private sector must work together to ensure a just and rapid transformation to a net zero global economy. If we combine forces now, we can avert climate catastrophe.*[16]

Addressing the G20 Summit, PM Lee outlined three ways Singapore is preparing for the low-carbon transition: (1) harnessing technology and investing in low-carbon solutions; (2) scaling up sustainable finance, including through mobilising private capital through innovative financing solutions; and (3) strengthening international collaboration on sustainability initiatives including through cross-border power trade within the region.[17]

In February 2021, the Singapore Green Plan 2030 was unveiled — a whole-of-nation movement to advance Singapore's commitments under the UN's 2030 Sustainable Development Agenda and Paris Agreement. In the Association of Southeast Asian Nations (ASEAN), there is now growing regional collaboration on sustainability initiatives to unlock the large and mutually beneficial economic opportunities in the push for decarbonisation and sustainability. For example, Singapore is working to establish regional power grids with ASEAN neighbours. The Lao People's Democratic Republic (PDR)–Thailand–Malaysia–Singapore Power Integration Project (LTMS-PIP) will facilitate cross-border power trade within the region.

---

[16] UNFCCC, "Secretary-General's Statement on the IPCC Working Group 1 Report on the Physical Science Basis of the Sixth Assessment," August 9, 2021, https://unfccc.int/news/secretary-general-s-statement-on-the-ipcc-working-group-1-report-on-the-physical-science-basis-of.

[17] PMO, "Intervention by PM Lee Hsien Loong on 'Climate Change and Environment' at the G20 Rome Summit," October 31, 2021, https://www.pmo.gov.sg/Newsroom/Intervention-by-PM-Lee-Hsien-Loong-on-Climate-Change-and-Environment-at-the-G20-Rome-Summit.

However, only a third of businesses in Singapore say they are "strongly aligned" to the Singapore Green Plan 2030, while less than half are currently operating sustainably, according to the *Building A Greener Singapore* study conducted by Schneider Electric in 2021, which surveyed over 500 businesses and consumers each.[18] Businesses reported funding difficulties, due to the financial and economic fallout of the pandemic, and changing the culture of the company as major barriers faced in turning green strategies into action. The key motivators for businesses to move towards a low-carbon economy were found to be government regulations, climate-related risk and financial market pressure.[19] However, consumers surveyed appeared to expect businesses to do more in this respect. Nine out of 10 Singaporeans support the country transitioning away from fossil fuels in its energy generation, but only around half were willing to pay higher prices for cleaner electricity as cost and convenience were topmost concerns when it came to greener living.[20]

World leaders and representatives at the COP26 summit have made promises to curb deforestation, phase down coal, end funding for fossil fuels abroad and cut methane emissions. Some 450 financial organisations, which between them control $130 trillion, agreed to back "clean" technology and direct finance away from fossil fuel industries.[21] Singapore has joined the Powering Past Coal Alliance, a coalition of 137 countries and businesses promoting the transition from coal to clean energy, and Minister for Sustainability and the Environment Grace Fu promoted and co-facilitated Article 6 of COP26 on the global carbon market. Nonetheless, there is still a significant gap between the measures countries

---

[18] Wallace Woon, "A Third of Businesses Here 'Strongly Aligned' With Singapore Green Plan 2030: Study," *The Straits Times*, October 12, 2021, https://www.straitstimes.com/singapore/environment/a-third-of-businesses-here-strongly-aligned-with-singapore-green-plan-2030; Schneider Electric, "Building A Greener Singapore," October 12, 2021, https://www.se.com/sg/en/download/document/Building-a-Greener-SG, 6.

[19] Ibid., 10.

[20] Ibid., 14.

[21] Simon Jessop and Andrea Shalal, "COP26 Coalition Worth $130 Trillion Vows to Put Climate at Heart of Finance," *Reuters*, November 4, 2021, https://www.reuters.com/business/cop/wrapup-politicians-exit-cop26-130tn-worth-financiers-take-stage-2021-11-03.

have committed to and what is needed to avoid more than 1.5 degrees Celsius of warming, beyond which the worst consequences of climate change will be felt.

For the young, whose future is at stake, it is a race against time. Youth movements everywhere are demanding urgent climate action. We are witnessing huge youth-led social movements unfolding, community by community and facilitated by social media and strengthened by transnational solidarity. During the COP26 summit, youth rallies were organised as part of a "Global Day of Action for Climate Justice".[22] Over 100,000 people marched in Glasgow to demand more action on the climate crisis, alongside 100 climate change demonstrations in 100 other countries. These young climate activists are using their moral authority as children and social media influence to rise against a system they regard as being aware of the climate emergency but not acting in emergency to protect their future.

Societal pressure and collaboration are vital in the push for change. The call of the young is loud and clear. But let us not leave it to our children to cry out and pressure collective action to secure the future.

Women as Game Changers in Our Normative Struggle

Women, better than anyone, understand the struggle for our normative future, establishing new norms and agendas to dismantle entrenched discrimination. From the birth of the UN Charter, which promises "the equal rights of men and women", women participated actively in the multilateral space to address widespread gender inequality in legal, social and economic rights. They pursued a strategy of "inside-outside partnership" to mobilise both the resources of the UN and of civil society to change patriarchal norms and social arrangements, and put difficult issues on the UN agenda to improve our human prospects. In particular, the four global United Nations Conferences on Women in Mexico (1975), Copenhagen (1980), Nairobi (1985) and Beijing (1995), with the theme

---

[22] COP26 Coalition, "Global Day of Action for Climate Justice," https://cop26coalition.org/gda.

"Equality, Development and Peace" culminating in the Beijing Declaration and Platform for Action, catalysed change for women in country after country.

Let me share three examples of women as game changers when they were given leadership positions in the UN. Helvi Sipilä from Finland was the first woman to hold the position of UN Assistant Secretary-General in 1972. She used her position to organise the first ever World Conference on Women in Mexico three years later. This opened up new spaces for women everywhere to connect the aspirations of local people to global institutions and the international community. When Dr Nafis Sadik from Pakistan was appointed as the first woman from the developing world to head an operational fund of the UN as the Executive Director of the United Nations Population Fund (UNFPA) in 1987, she brought a whole new narrative and perspective to population and development issues. Till then, the men were too afraid to talk about sex when it came to population issues. Dr Sadik, supported by women civil society actors, forced open the curtains and doors to reveal the scale of maternal mortality and the need to address sexual and reproductive health of women in population policies and programmes. Inspired by these women leaders, I myself as head of the United Nations Development Fund for Women (UNIFEM), supported by civil society, worked with the UN Security Council to establish Security Council Resolution (SCR) 1325 on Women, Peace and Security, which criminalised the use of sexual violence as a weapon of war, and addressed the importance of women's perspectives and participation in decision-making for sustainable peace.

Coming out of patriarchal societies, women wanted nothing less than the transformation of the 21st century to ensure that daughters had the same opportunities as sons; that women could realise their rights to quality education, employment and healthcare; that women would not be undervalued, overworked and underpaid; that there is recognition and social support for women's caregiving roles; that they have equal citizenship rights and would be free from violent conflicts, harassment and sexual violence. From the beginning, women knew that they had to be the primary agents of this transformation.

By using the values and platform of multilateral governance, women seized the opportunity for change and strived to achieve the transformation needed on a global scale to sustain the change. Women game changers unleashed their power to foster a "people-centred multilateralism", and in the words of Ralph Bunche when drafting the UN Charter, "make change — even radical change — possible without violent upheaval".[23]

I am pleased that in 2021, Singapore has embraced an inclusive society based on gender equality. From September 2020 to September 2021, more than 100 dialogues with over 5,000 participants have reviewed issues affecting women, as more Singaporeans realise the importance of engaging women, valuing women's experiences and expertise as a pathway to a more sustainable and caring future.[24] Leaders globally are becoming more aware of the importance of removing gender barriers for both men and women to unleash the expertise and power of the female half of humanity to balance the male, to change the trajectory of vulnerability, and to co-create the wellbeing of people and planet.

In this age of great disruptions, we are standing at the threshold of the future. Like the proverbial Angel of History, our eyes are turned towards the past and present, even as we are propelled towards the future by the "storm of progress".[25] What does the Angel of History see — a garden in an earthly paradise or a wasteland of rubble at the edge of a dark abyss? What we choose to do now, to our own species and our planet, will not only profoundly shape our future, but remain as a testament of our history.

---

[23] Ralph Bunche, "Some Reflections on Peace in Our Time," Nobel lecture delivered at the University of Oslo, December 11, 1950, https://www.nobelprize.org/prizes/peace/1950/bunche/lecture.

[24] REACH, "Conversations on Singapore Women's Development," accessed December 20, 2021, https://www.reach.gov.sg/Participate/conversations-on-singapore-womens-development.

[25] Walter Benjamin, "On the Concept of History (1940)," trans. Dennis Redmond, accessed December 20, 2021, https://www.marxists.org/reference/archive/benjamin/1940/history.htm.

The UN has served as the platform for collective action, norm development and international cooperation, to solve the problems that matter most to our human existence. However, the UN alone can no longer address the numerous challenges confronting us in our complex and networked world. In my next lecture, I will discuss our common agenda and a renewed multilateralism to secure our future, and how Singapore can contribute to this breakthrough that may lead us towards "a garden in an earthly paradise".

Question-and-Answer Session
Moderated by Professor Tommy Koh

Dr Noeleen Heyzer speaking with Professor Tommy Koh at her Q&A session
Source: Jacky Ho for the Institute of Policy Studies

Professor Tommy Koh: I want to begin by thanking Noeleen for having delivered a very important lecture with great eloquence and passion. Your lecture has two parts. The first part is about four great disruptions — the COVID-19 pandemic and future pandemics, the climate crisis, the digital revolution and armed conflict. The second part of your lecture is about building our normative future.

So my first question to you is: What are the norms which you think are important for us to uphold as we face the future? When I listened to you, I identified seven norms: equality, inclusion, sustainability, resilience, human rights and gender equality, good governance and trustworthy government, and finally, international cooperation and multilateralism.

Dr Noeleen Heyzer: Absolutely.

Prof Koh: You don't mind if I challenge you?

Dr Heyzer: But I will have to challenge you back, Prof Koh.

Prof Koh: In the course of your wonderful lecture, you talked about the very unsatisfactory situation in the world concerning vaccines. You said that 10 rich countries in the world possess 95 per cent of the total vaccines that we have. And both António Guterres and Dr Tedros have used very strong words to describe the situation. Tedros called it "vaccine apartheid" and the WHO has condemned countries like Singapore that have given booster shots to the population. The reason is that there are so many people in the world who have not yet received even the single first shot. So my question to you is this: Are Tedros and António making unreasonable demands? Considering that we live in a world of nation states, and naturally every government will look after the welfare of its own people first. The Prime Minister of Singapore will buy vaccines for his own people first before he would donate them to other countries, right? I mean, this is realism.

Dr Heyzer: Yes.

Prof Koh: So one has to balance realism and idealism. The idealistic situation would be if vaccines were freely available to the 7 billion people in the world. But that's not the kind of world we live in. What is your own position?

Dr Heyzer: Let us look at some of the ideas behind your question. I personally feel that it is important for countries to protect their population.

The issue is not just about access to vaccines, it is about the production of vaccines. It is about intellectual property (IP) rights, basically. And the fact that there are developing countries that have the capacity to produce more vaccines and be helped in this area. So instead of just looking at countries that have vaccines, we have to encourage more production of vaccines and their distribution.

Prof Koh: Do you realise that the government doesn't own the vaccines? The vaccines were invented and manufactured by private commercial entities and they have IP rights. I mean, they're not charities, they are pharmaceutical companies. Of course, we are very grateful to them that in such a short time they have come up with so many effective vaccines. So what are you proposing?

Dr Heyzer: That's why I asked this question in my lecture: Is our 21st-century capitalism adequate if we are going to make global public health a public good?

The main reason is that I think in the long run, these companies will have to be aware that it is a case of having short-term versus long-term interests. Can these companies, in a way, not make so much profit and instead ask how much they are willing to invest in sustainability? To not see it as a cost or as not making enough profits for their shareholders, but really looking at the fact that they have stakeholders who care about sustainability issues and who want to have a future. So I think at the end of the day, there needs to be a conversation. We can't just decide on something; we have to develop the analysis, understand what are the trade-offs and then learn that what we may see as trade-offs are in fact not trade-offs but part of a synergetic framework of decision-making. That's my hope, Prof Koh. I may be a bit too idealistic but I honestly hope that the current corporate governance structure, and their enlightened people who act out of self-interest, will see solidarity as self-interest.

Prof Koh: But you must also understand that if you're a pharmaceutical company and you've invested billions of dollars in research and development, that you would like to be able to recover the investment and make some money for your shareholders.

Dr Heyzer: Yes. The only thing is this — they have also benefited from the investment of our countries, nation states and a more stable global order. It's not like it's just the technical knowledge of the production of these vaccines. It is the fact that we have helped to maintain a stable world order that helps us function as a human community. It is the idea that there is not enough valuing of what have secured our world; my hope is that we begin valuing our future slightly differently. It's going to be a long run; it's not something that will happen overnight.

Prof Koh: So are you saying that pharmaceutical companies like Pfizer and Moderna should waive their IP rights?

Dr Heyzer: I think the World Trade Organization (WTO) has some arrangements whereby they allow countries to actually manufacture some of the cheap drugs, such as for HIV/AIDs. So there are certain arrangements that can be made without having to waive IP rights entirely. And I think this requires more imaginative thinking. It's not an either-or thing or a black-and-white thing. I would actually challenge people to come together to actually say: How can we best address this major issue? Are there other ways of going about it?

Prof Koh: In fact, President Biden has said that he was willing to waive the IP rights to the vaccine, but he doesn't own the IP rights. The European Union, on the other hand, said that they opposed the proposal to waive IP rights. And their argument is not without validity, which is that it's not just about IP rights. You need the scientific know-how, infrastructure and time, before you can actually produce this vaccine. Even if somebody were to give you the formula, it doesn't mean that you'd be able to produce it, right?

Dr Heyzer: Absolutely.

Prof Koh: So do you agree with Tedros in his condemnation of countries for giving their people booster shots?

Dr Heyzer: I don't agree with him fully because I think if we need booster shots, we need booster shots.

Prof Koh: If your vantage point is global equity, then you should be against booster shots.

Dr Heyzer: No, I'm hoping that we will create greater cooperation. In other words, don't look at it as a contained amount of vaccines. I honestly think we should be producing more and have more networks of production centres. And not, of course, go to countries where they don't have the capacity of production, but more so to invest in countries that have the capacities or whose capacities can be strengthened. So, it's to not see it as a closed circle. That is my hope. I know it's not going to be easy but I am a very hopeful person.

Prof Koh: Let's take questions from the audience.

Participant: Thanks Noeleen for a lovely lecture. Your great disruptions are quite a bleak analysis of what the world is facing. I just wanted to say one thing. I think what the world today is lacking is global leadership. If we look at what happened after the world wars, it was the leadership of the US that brought the world order to what it was, to what it has been for a long time. But now, they are looking inward and riddled by all types of problems. And we don't have any other country which is coming up; China is still a bit leery about taking this global leadership position. So in this scenario, how do we hope that the world can emerge stronger?

Prof Koh: Do you think Biden is providing the world with the leadership it needs?

Dr Heyzer: Once upon a time, we needed very powerful superpowers to shape the world and provide the type of guarantees that we needed. I think now, it is much more difficult because power is much dispersed. And it's not just even within nation states. We now have multilateral corporations who actually own greater wealth than some countries and in fact, may wield greater power. And not only multilateral corporations, but wealthy individuals as well. So the world has changed and become more dispersed, and power has also been much dispersed and occurs in different forms.

Now, the thing is, we still very much have a state-based way of organising multilateral governance. However, one of the things that came out of the common agenda that the UN Secretary-General put forth in the last General Assembly was a network of inclusive multilateralism. And that in a sense has allowed us to ask: What type of problems are we facing? Who can bring forth the solutions to these specific problems? Who has the power to deal with this specific set of issues?

So I don't think we need to wait until the emergence of another powerful state. I like the idea of, and I've always worked from it, multilateralism from the ground up. And what that means is to start with what are the problems faced, because there's so many and they're so complex. We just talked about vaccines and look how complex it is. If we are to look at climate change, there are just so many different parts of it. Who can provide the solutions to these problems and who has the power to do so? I see it as an alliance of action, to start from the ground and then bring in very powerful people, including states, to make that type of decision. In fact, for a while, we thought that it was the G20, then we thought of having the 3G to make sure that the G20 doesn't run away with their own agenda but that everybody is included. These are all innovations, and I think it is time to be very innovative. We obviously have the threat of great disruptions but I honestly think that we also have the human imagination to do it.

Prof Koh: To summarise your reply, we live in a new world and maybe in this new world you do not need the leadership of one powerful country but a network of like-minded leaders from governments, cities, the private sector, civil society and so on.

Let me read you two other questions that have come in. For international multilateral organisations, is it possible to weigh the interests of the most powerful members against other less powerful members? And the next question is about the erosion of trust. The question is: How do we rebuild trust between people and the government and authorities and so on?

Dr Heyzer: Let me start with the second question on trust. Why has trust been broken? Trust has been broken because people feel that there's a sense of unfairness. Trust has been broken because people expect certain things from leadership. Trust has been broken because when people go to work they expect that the workplace will be safe and that they will be allowed to work productively, and so on and so forth. If we are to rebuild trust, we need to understand what matters most to people. And not just the powerful and the elites; different people have different interests. And most of the time, the people who are struggling want very basic things — human security, protection against harassment, the capacity to dream for their children, the ladders of upward social mobility, hope that the next generation can live better than this generation. It's not that difficult.

And let's not forget what matters most to our planet as well. We can't just leave the planet out of this equation; it is our home. So if we look at what matters most, it is about protection and participation, because people want agency as well. Many don't even want handouts, it's not like "Oh, you know what you need, we give it to you and you stay quiet." People want the sense that they are empowered, they want a sense of dignity. Give people dignity, so that they can actually celebrate and flourish in the human context. So I think these are all things that will build trust, and we need to have the right institutions, the right leadership and the accountable use of power. And power for whom? It's not "power over", I think we have to break out of the concept of "power over"; it should be "power with". How can we use "power with" to allow others to flourish as much as we flourish ourselves? I think that this practice is going to be very new because we are not there yet.

In terms of the interests of powerful countries versus less powerful countries, the problem currently is that the powerful countries are involved with geopolitical rivalry of different sorts. The less powerful countries are trying to find a space of neutrality so that they're not caught in the type of world that we experienced during the Cold War that had a very high human toll, unfortunately. So, I think what will bring us together is to find areas of common interests, where we can build solidarity, and to have a framework of action. Where can we act together for our collective future and our common agenda? Where do we need to compete? Because I'm an idealist but also a realist spinning towards the idealistic world, if you like.

Where are the areas we are competing in? Where are the areas that we totally disagree with because we have very different normative frameworks? How do we manage that? Unfortunately we are living at a time where if we don't manage this properly, we actually have in our power weapons of self-destruction, our nuclear power, which can destroy the whole of human existence. We need to be extremely careful on how we deal with that area of work. So I would say, let's build where we can in the areas where we have common interests and look at solidarity as self-interest. As I stressed in my first lecture, what helped to develop our multilateral world 76 years ago was the coming together of people with different interests who actually saw solidarity as self-interest and built the framework and pathway to move forward. And I think that we are at that stage, the Angel of History, where we have to look into the past and the present, and also into the future.

Prof Koh: I would give a different answer. I would say that we will always live in an unequal world because there are big countries and small countries, rich countries and not-so-rich countries, and the world will always favour the big and the strong.

But those who are small and less powerful can organise themselves. So one of the good things that Singapore had done is that 29 years ago, we took the initiative to organise the small countries and created the FOSS. Today, the FOSS has 108 members, which is the majority of UN membership.

Dr Heyzer: Absolutely.

Prof Koh: And by being together it gives us collective strength. It amplifies our voice, gives us leverage in negotiating with big countries and gives smaller countries a better chance of getting elected to UN bodies. But the world is still unequal, it will always be unequal, but I think the FOSS has helped to make it a little less unequal.

Dr Heyzer: I fully agree with you, Prof Koh. In fact, this is what the women's movement has been doing. Individually we are so weak, but we are powerful as a movement — look at the type of changes we've been able to bring about. This is because of transnational mobilisation and organisation, which I think is important.

Prof Koh: Let me ask you a final question. This participant said that some people have suggested that the World Bank should be repurposed for the sole task of climate change. Do you agree?

Dr Heyzer: I think the World Bank should be helping with climate action but not forget the work on ending poverty. Development is absolutely critical. I was so shocked at the figure that 97 million people are falling into poverty again. So I would say, please don't forget development.

Prof Koh: So I guess our reply is that the World Bank's work is not yet done, but that climate change should also be part of your agenda.

Dr Heyzer: Absolutely right.

Prof Koh: Noeleen, please share with us a concluding remark that we can take away from this inspiring session.

Dr Heyzer: I will leave it to you, Prof Koh. You are the source of wisdom and my mentor, so I will allow you to say the concluding remark and I will go along with it.

Prof Koh: This is passing the buck, you know! So let me speak on Noeleen's behalf and say that the world faces four existential threats — the current pandemic and future pandemic, the climate crisis, the dark side of the digital revolution and never-ending armed conflict. We want to recover from these to prevent further crises, but we want to do it in the right way. And we want to do it in a way that's based upon norms that we all support. Some of these norms have been articulated by Noeleen — equality, inclusion, human rights, gender equality, good governance, trustworthy government and putting the individual, no matter how humble, at the core of everything that we do.

Dr Heyzer: Absolutely. And with that Prof Koh, I will have to add one more thing. I promised my dear friend Janet Lim because I talked about forced displacement in my lecture. She's very concerned about the number of people who are displaced at this time and her wish, and I think it is so important for us to really reflect on this. She said that Singapore is now such a rich country, what else can we do in terms of technical support, educational support, financial support globally but also in our neighbourhood to support the displacement of people, the forced displacement of refugees and of undocumented migrants? And that is something, because we tend to forget about the most disadvantaged, and that is something I just want to share as a final thought.

Thank you Prof Koh for this wonderful session.

Prof Koh: Thank you, please join me in congratulating Noeleen.

Lecture III
SECURING OUR FUTURE: A RENEWED MULTILATERALISM

LECTURE III

This final lecture is titled "Securing Our Future: A Renewed Multilateralism". We went on a journey to the past and present in my first and second lecture. My third lecture will turn our gaze to the horizon of the future.

As the Danish philosopher Søren Kierkegaard once said: "Life can only be understood backwards; but it must be lived forwards."[1] With an understanding of history from the standpoint of our present, we must safeguard our world and nurture the seeds of our collective future. We are living through a time every bit as momentous as that faced by our forefathers and mothers seven decades ago. Our generation is tasked with nothing less than the rejuvenation of the world, in all aspects — natural, political, economic, social and cultural. We must acknowledge the underlying interconnectedness of the universe, of human life and the natural world, not merely as a philosophical concept; we must realise this interconnectedness deep in our bones, and apply this principle of interconnectedness to the very structures that govern our lived reality.

---

[1] Søren Kierkegaard, "Journal JJ," in *Kierkegaard's Journals and Notebooks, Volume 2: Journals EE-KK* (Princeton: Princeton University Press, 2008), 179.

At the level of international governance, we need to rejuvenate the multilateral rule-based order to secure our future. We will be defined by how we respond to this call of destiny. As we look towards the future that our children and grandchildren will inherit, we must ask what kind of world and what kind of society we want to be — and how we can achieve it.

In my first two lectures, I talked about the framework of multilateral governance that has secured our present but now needs to be renewed and strengthened to deal with the interlocking disruptions that threaten our future. What is to be done? To secure our future requires an awareness that trust and solidarity, the rope that holds society together from the local to the global, is unravelling. We are connected more than ever by our vulnerability and the need to value our future differently. To have the future we want, we must *repair, restore* and *revalue*. Repair what has been broken — trust and solidarity; restore what has been weakened — protection and dignity; and revalue what has been ignored — caring for each other and the planet. This must be done globally through multilateral governance, and locally by our countries, corporations and alliances of people, especially the young, who are empowered by technology to build a transnational community based on shared values and a shared purpose to magnify the good and diminish the bad.

The Foundation of Our Global Future

The foundation of our global future is clearly outlined in the *Our Common Agenda* report by UN Secretary-General António Guterres. Leaders of the world identified 12 areas for urgent action and requested the Secretary-General to report back to the General Assembly with recommendations "to advance our common agenda and to respond to current and future challenges".[2] I will highlight what I see in *Our Common Agenda* as the three most important ways to rebuild the foundations of our global future: a renewed social contract; governance of our global commons and global public goods; and an inclusive-networked-effective multilateralism.

---

[2] UN, *Our Common Agenda — Report of the Secretary-General* (New York: United Nations, 2021), 14.

A Renewed Social Contract

Our Common Agenda places trust and solidarity at its core to allow the community of nations to work together again to achieve common goals. The UN Secretary-General has urgently called for a renewed social contract built on three foundations necessary for the 21st century: trust; inclusion, protection and participation; and measuring and valuing what matters to people and the planet.

The renewed social contract seeks to secure a future where trust is rebuilt as people see results reflected in their daily lives, confident that the system is working for them. For this to happen, global and national systems must deliver what people need most. It is vital that updated governance arrangements deliver better public goods and "usher in a new era of universal social protection, health coverage, education, skills, decent work and housing, as well as universal access to the Internet by 2030 as a basic human right".[3]

A vibrant social contract guarantees the conditions for people to live a decent life by building the foundations for social sustainability and social security, especially inclusion, protection and participation for people and communities left behind. Measuring and valuing what matters to people and the planet requires broad shifts in what prosperity and progress mean, capturing the human and environmental destruction of some business activities, and changing our economic models to value the systems that sustain life and well-being. It must also find ways to validate the care and informal economy done by women, and invest in quality paid care as part of essential public services and social protection arrangements. Underpinning the social contract is the centrality of human rights. Human rights are vital problem-solving tools that safeguard lives and livelihoods and are critical to sustaining peace, as they prevent grievances from arising. They serve the whole of society, not just the individual. To implement the renewed social contract requires a whole-of-society approach, as many more actors are

---
[3] Ibid., 4.

needed to address increasingly complex and interconnected problems. Countries are encouraged to conduct inclusive and meaningful national consultations so all citizens have a say in envisioning their countries' future.

Governance of the Global Commons and Global Public Goods

To complement the renewed social contract, *Our Common Agenda* calls for a "new global deal" to enhance the governance of the global commons and global public goods.[4] The global commons refer to natural or cultural resources that are shared by and benefit all. They include the oceans, polar regions, atmosphere and outer space. Public goods are understood to be those goods and services provided to and benefiting all of society. Certain public goods are global in nature as they cannot be adequately provided by any one state acting alone and they concern the welfare of humanity. These include global public health, the global economy, a healthy planet, peace and security, and the digital commons. Having addressed global public health and a healthy planet in my second lecture, I will now focus on the global economy, peace and security, and the digital commons.

A Global Economy That Works for All

A global economy that works for all, that is sustainable and equitable, has characteristics of a global public good. Achieving this new dynamic for the global economy means rethinking the interdependence between the economy, people and planet. Strong and sustainable businesses are built on global values — including human and labour rights, environmental sustainability, and anti-corruption. Increasingly, global businesses are under pressure to find drivers of growth that do not damage our social fabric, cultural heritage or the environment for future generations. Environment, social and governance (ESG) factors are used today as criteria for socially responsible investing. In the wake of the global economic crisis and a steady

---

[4] UN, "New Global Deal that Shares Power, Resources Would Be Crucial in Building Just, Sustainable Future, Secretary-General Tells World Summit for Social Development," December 1, 2020, https://www.un.org/press/en/2020/sgsm20465.doc.htm.

stream of corporate scandals, crises of corporate governance have pushed ESG from the margins to the boardrooms of corporations, integrated into corporate management and operations. Coordinated action by the business community to align their business practices with global goals, including the Paris Climate Agreement and the Sustainable Development Goals (SDGs), is crucial. World leaders and civil society have expressed their belief that responsible business practices will be critical to restoring public trust in the global financial and economic system.

Stronger global cooperation to promote financial integrity by addressing tax evasion, aggressive tax avoidance, as well as illicit financial flows is long overdue. Measures to increase fairness — such as a minimum global corporate tax and solidarity tax — would be clear signals that private enterprises and the very wealthy who benefit most from current economic arrangements must contribute to national and global public goods.

New Threats to Peace and Security

Peace is a principal global public good that the UN was established to deliver. Today's risks to collective peace and security are growing and traditional forms of conflict prevention, management and resolution are ill-suited to address the emerging dangers. This includes conflicts involving transnational criminal networks, new actors associated with terrorism, rapidly evolving weapon technologies and a willingness of regional actors to participate directly in wars. New technologies have placed the capacity to disrupt global stability in the hands of many more actors. Longstanding agreements on nuclear weapons and other weapons of mass destruction are increasingly fragile as trust among major powers continues to erode. The world is moving closer to the brink of instability, where the risks we face are no longer managed effectively through the systems we have.

The UN Secretary-General has set out a new agenda for peace. To protect and manage the global public good of peace, we need a peace continuum based on a better understanding of the underlying drivers and systems of influence that are generating and sustaining conflict, a renewed effort to agree on more effective collective security responses and a meaningful set of steps to manage emerging risks. This means investing in prevention and building the infrastructure of peace, ensuring adequate social spending, decent work and development assistance to address root causes of conflict and upholding human rights. It means reducing strategic risks by the effective control of conventional weapons and the regulation of new weapons of technology; banning cyberattacks on civilian infrastructure, putting in place measures to de-escalate cyber-related risks, and establishing internationally agreed limits on lethal autonomous weapons systems. It requires deepening support for regional capacities, including security arrangements and joint peacebuilding cooperation to address complex peace and security challenges. The Peace Agenda also calls for a multi-stakeholder effort to reduce violence significantly worldwide and in all its forms, including against women and girls, building on the movement to halve global violence by 2030.

Reclaiming the Digital Commons

Our world is changing beyond recognition, as we move from the industrial age to the hyperconnected digital age. The Internet has provided access to information for billions, fostering collaboration, connection and mobilisation for sustainable development. It is a global public good that should benefit everyone, everywhere. Today, however, the potential harms of the digital domain risk overshadowing its benefits. Governance at the national and global levels has not kept pace with the inherently informal and decentralised nature of the Internet, which is dominated by commercial interests. Serious and urgent ethical, social and regulatory questions confront us, including the lack of accountability in the cyberspace and the emergence of large technology companies as geopolitical actors. At the same time, there is gender bias, as women do not have an equal role in designing digital technologies and algorithms. Meanwhile, digital harassment has targeted women and girls and pushed many women out of the public conversation. There is also real concern over the use of digital surveillance and manipulation to influence behaviour and control populations.

To protect the online space and strengthen its governance, the UN will soon be organising a multi-stakeholder digital technology track in preparation for a Summit of the Future in 2023 to agree on a Global Digital Compact.[5] This will outline shared principles for an open, free and secure digital future for all. Complex digital issues that could be addressed include reaffirming the fundamental commitment to connecting the unconnected, avoiding the fragmentation of the Internet, providing people with options on how their data is used, applying human rights online and promoting a trustworthy Internet by introducing accountability criteria for discrimination and misleading content. More broadly, the Global Digital Compact could also promote the regulation of artificial intelligence (AI) to ensure that it is aligned with shared global values.

Success in finding solutions to the interlinked problems we face hinges on our ability to anticipate, prevent and prepare for major risks to come. These risks are now increasingly global, some even existential as the nuclear age has given humanity the power to bring about its own extinction. Continued technological advances, accelerating climate change, transnational security threats and new pandemics mean that the likelihood of global catastrophe is present on multiple fronts. The UN Secretary-General has put a revitalised prevention agenda front and centre in all that we do. Being prepared to prevent and respond to these risks is an essential counterpoint to better manage the global commons and global public goods. These are all actions that the UN will be deliberating with member states, in close consultation with other relevant stakeholders at the Summit of the Future in 2023 during the 78th UN General Assembly. The expected outcome is agreement on the renewed social contract, and identification of those global commons or public goods that may require renewed commitments and governance.

---

[5] UN, *Our Common Agenda — Report of the Secretary-General* (New York: United Nations, 2021), 7.

Networked-Inclusive-Effective Multilateralism

The world has changed since the UN was founded, and so must multilateral governance to be effective. When the UN Charter was developed, multilateralism meant cooperation among 51 member states with the United States (US) as the centre of power. Today, there are 193 member states, and a shift in global power from West to East. The context for collective action has evolved over the past seven decades, with a broader range of state and non-state actors participating in global affairs. There is a diffusion of power extending to a whole host of networks and institutions that inhabit the fabric of global society. Today, we are witnessing the growing power of multinational corporations, along with ultra-rich individuals. There are thousands of non-government organisations, networks and citizens' movements using social media to extend their reach and amplify the voices of citizens and civil society. At the same time, in our hyperconnected world, what happens in one nation can impact all nations. Any effort to improve our governance of the global commons and public goods and to manage risks must navigate this complexity and seek explicitly to incorporate new approaches where they are likely to deliver better outcomes. What might this mean in practice? It means all global stakeholders realising that solidarity is self-interest and taking greater collective responsibility for managing the global commons and global public goods, and the great disruptions of the 21st century. These are issues that no country can address alone. They require the concerted resolve of all stakeholders working together — governments, cities, corporations, civil society and even private citizens.

While the UN alone cannot address the numerous challenges confronting humanity, especially in a complex and networked world, it is still the key institution available for solving the problems that matter most. The UN has legitimacy and universal convening power that gives all 193 member states an equal voice, increasingly joined by representatives from the private sector, civil society and academia. It has a unique role in safeguarding global values, ethics and norms as well as a global presence and technical expertise. However, the UN of the 20th century must change into the UN of the 21st century, to become a reliable guardian for our future, acting on behalf of both the present and succeeding generation.

An improved multilateral governance focuses on protecting our global commons and delivering critical global public goods, as well as being prepared to respond to major risks in a more networked and inclusive world by improving collaboration and strategic engagement with other actors. Networked and inclusive multilateralism suggests a paradigm shift from the state-centric international world order to one where myriad actors, beyond nation-states (especially beyond traditional major powers), can collaboratively share and implement solutions to complex problems. They all emphasised the need for alliances between state and non-state actors — or "smart coalitions" — to respond as a "people-centred and people-driven multilateralism" to transnational challenges calling for a stronger sense of global community, solidarity and responsibility.

Multilateralism that is more networked draws together existing institutional capacities, overcoming fragmentation to ensure all are working together towards a common goal. It solves problems by drawing on the capacities and hearing the voices of all relevant actors — rather than being driven by mandates or institutions alone. In a networked world, the UN is an important convener: a place to build consensus around priorities and strategies, and a platform for collective action and delivery. It is the space to bring together decision-makers with the accountability and authoritativeness associated with intergovernmental processes to support networked approaches. It must do this better, and more often.

Inclusive multilateralism is marked by a genuine possibility for states from all regions and of all sizes to engage in collective action, including a stronger voice for developing countries in global decision-making. It also means the inclusion of a diverse range of voices beyond states in addition to intergovernmental organisations. This can include parliaments, subnational authorities (cities and local governments), civil society, faith-based organisations, universities, trade unions, the private sector and grassroots movements, including those led by women and young people. This vision recognises that states remain central to our collective ability to meet global challenges and have unique responsibilities in the multilateral system, while also acknowledging that solutions increasingly depend on the private sector and non-state actors, which should be part of the deliberations and be accountable for their commitments.

Ultimately, what matters is results. For the UN to be more effective, it needs to be nimble and dynamic, able to respond to volatile situations and new emergencies. There is no way to anticipate which extreme risk event will come next; it might be another pandemic, a new war, a biological attack, a cyberattack on critical infrastructure, technological developments gone awry and unconstrained by ethical and regulatory frameworks.

The Secretary-General has proposed the establishment of an Emergency Platform to respond to complex global crises.[6] The platform would be triggered automatically in crises of sufficient scale and magnitude, regardless of the type or nature of the crisis involved. Once activated, it would bring together leaders from member states, the UN system, key country groupings, international financial institutions, regional bodies, civil society, the private sector, subject-specific industries and other experts. The platform would allow the convening role of the Secretary-General to be maximised in the face of crises with global reach.

A new multilateral governance that is more networked, inclusive and effective will require every nation to rethink how we grow our economy, mediate and negotiate our differences, share our wealth, nurture our environment, and care for the well-being of our population. It is essential to engage the private sector to shift the needle significantly on critical challenges, inclusion and accountability. Arrangements where the private sector commits to business models that support inclusion, empowerment, human rights and sustainable development, and investments that take into account ESG factors, are important in this regard.

---

[6] Ibid.

What might these new alliances look like in practice and what kind of impact can they actually have? The good news is that there are several innovative and forward-looking public–private partnerships already addressing critical challenges while creating opportunities and delivering dividends for communities. One such example is the TRANSFORM initiative, a social enterprise support platform created by Unilever and the United Kingdom's Foreign, Commonwealth and Development Office, which aims to help 100 million people in Sub-Saharan Africa and South Asia gain access to products and services that improve health, livelihoods, the environment or well-being by 2025. TRANSFORM works to accelerate community enterprises; blending funding and support to deliver market-based solutions to the world's biggest development challenges. So far, TRANSFORM has reached around 4 million people from low-income communities in 13 countries around the world.[7] With the engagement of an impressive network of partners, including Microsoft, Mastercard and LinkedIn, TRANSFORM has supported 56 "impact enterprise" projects, including a mobile e-commerce platform in Rwanda, a women and maternal health information service in Nigeria, and affordable water and sanitation providers in Bangladesh and India. One project, Dharma Life in India, provided mentoring and support to a network of over 16,000 rural women to become village level entrepreneurs to facilitate access to vital information, goods and services to vulnerable communities during the COVID-19 pandemic, transforming them into a women-led grassroots crisis response force that delivers to the last mile.

We need to learn from such innovations and the concrete impacts they can make. Revitalised relationships and alliances for inclusive and sustainable development can harness the ideas and talents of the public, private, civil society, faith groups and citizens everywhere, uniting around problems and generating solutions to secure our common future. However, they can only be built if they are based on shared values, visions and goals

---

[7] Transform, "Our Portfolio," November 2020, https://www.transform.global/wp-content/uploads/2020/11/TRANSFORM-portfolio-overview-Nov20.pdf.

on managing global public risks, the long-term governance of the global commons and delivery of global public goods. These are not abstract concepts; they lie at the very heart of the community, be it at the local, national or international level.

Securing Singapore's Future: An Epicentre of Multilateralism?

There are many ways in which Singapore can become an epicentre of multilateralism, securing its future by contributing to the larger well-being of people and the planet. Let me reflect on three: a hub for global public health, a digital hub for cybersecurity and a financial hub for an inclusive and sustainable future.

Hub for Global Public Health

Singapore has played an important role in global health security during the COVID-19 pandemic, as shared in my second lecture. It can now be more ambitious and become a hub for global public health in three ways: linking public health to environmental health, improving health equity in healthcare delivery and taking advantage of frontier healthcare technology.

Singapore can use the sustainable development paradigm to take leadership and become a multilateral hub for global public health, one that understands the social and environmental determinants of health to improve the conditions and quality of people's daily lives. It means understanding that every sector is a health sector, that an empowered society is a healthy society and just having medical care is not enough. Seen through the prism of sustainable development, health is not the absence of illness but the presence of wellness, linked to the wellness of our ecological world and quality of our economic system and society. The 2030 Agenda for Sustainable Development is a development approach that integrates our economy, society and ecology to build resilience into the fabric of how communities function, empowering people to negotiate life. It balances the three dimensions of sustainable development: the economic, social and environmental, and regards them as integrated and interlinked in addressing new risks, vulnerabilities and opportunities. It is also about partnership for change and Singapore has already the experience of building a community of collaborators: governments, local leaders, civil society, business and academia to address various development agendas.

Singapore is already tracking its health systems interventions and how healthcare is delivered. New models of care in Singapore are moving from services that focus solely on treatment for people who are already ill towards services that work to improve the conditions in which people live and work. Approaches that focus on prevention and improving health equity will look quite different from those that focus on improving average population health, as they are responsive to communities with the greatest levels of need and people with the highest risks of poor health. This requires health sector–community collaboration for service delivery, access and affordability of treatment, and ways of addressing the social determinants of health to empower more people economically and socially to live healthy lives.

I had the opportunity to experience our healthcare services that support women who are the "older old" in low-income communities. From the Agency for Integrated Care to St. Hilda Community Services, to the Home Nursing Foundation, the nurses, the physiotherapists, the co-ordinators and the persons-in-charge have worked as a seamless collective. I was impressed with the support, training and equipment available for severely disabled elders in an old HDB estate with a large ageing population, restoring dignity to the vulnerable. This is an example of an innovation in community health governance that could be upscaled.

To become a hub for global public health, Singapore can further build on its human capacity and take advantage of innovation and frontier technology in healthcare. As healthcare goes digital, more healthcare will be delivered through smartphones. As mobile health (mHealth) gets more popular, we will be using more digital technology such as cheaper sensors, robotics and drones to reach people and deliver medicine to remote areas in Asia, and vulnerable communities including the displaced and refugees.

In its aim to be a digital hub of the future, Singapore can become a locally rooted global node that builds global public health governance and alliances that connect people and healthcare systems seamlessly through digital technology.

Digital Hub for Global Cybersecurity

The Asia-Pacific is predicted to become the leading region in terms of 5G technology adoption with some 1.2 billion users that would account for 65 per cent of global 5G users by 2024.[8] With Singapore's lead, the Association of Southeast Asian Nations (ASEAN) has also launched the ASEAN Smart Cities Network (ASCN) in 2018 to move ASEAN towards smart and sustainable urban development using digital technology.

While the adoption of 5G will enable wider implementation of Internet of Things (IoT) and robotics, it will also broaden the cyberattack surface. Critical infrastructure in Asia has already experienced multiple cyberattacks. Only a few ASEAN member states have issued regulations and guidelines to address Operational Technology (OT) cybersecurity to protect power stations, transport networks and smart city applications.

Because of differing levels of maturity for OT security policy across the Asia-Pacific region, there is a need for industry groups to take the lead in developing and harmonising best practices in cybersecurity. To prepare this section of the lecture, I asked the Director of Security Services of IBM for key recommendations. These are some of her recommendations: Singapore should focus on homegrown cybersecurity talent, have a mass drive of public awareness campaigns to address the weakest link — humans and have mandatory disclosures of cybersecurity ratings by the private sector.

I also visited the Global Cyber Security Operations of banking group Citi. They have provided guidance on policy development in individual

---

[8] GlobalData, "Asia-Pacific Will Lead 5G Technology Adoption by 2024, Says GlobalData," January 13, 2020, https://www.globaldata.com/asia-pacific-will-lead-5g-technology-adoption-2024-says-globaldata/aldata.com/asia-pacific-will-lead-5g-technology-adoption-2024-says-globaldata.

countries to address specific national or industrial needs. During their briefing, I asked them to identify the critical gaps that need to be addressed for Singapore to become the digital hub for global cybersecurity. They identified three. First, cybersecurity must be a priority on the national agenda. The future of growth and technology development in Singapore and the region requires cooperation and recognition that the information technology (IT) threat landscape has expanded. The threat landscape now includes personal mobile devices used for work, cloud technology, IoT technologies and connected OT devices. OT is critical not just for heavy industries, but also for today's highly connected smart cities. Second, there is an urgent need to build a pipeline of expertise in cybersecurity. This requires education to demystify cybersecurity and an understanding that a range of expertise beyond technological aspects is required for this sector to succeed. Third, as with most security infrastructure, there is a significant gender gap in cybersecurity. In the Asia-Pacific, women account for less than 10 per cent of the cybersecurity workforce.[9] This gap in women's participation has resulted in a lack of gender perspectives informing cybersecurity and the development of frameworks that fail to identify and respond to cyber threats faced by women and girls.

As countries seek to build a secure and resilient cyberspace, cybersecurity is unfortunately a male-dominated field in the world, leaving out the experiences and perspectives of half the world's population. In June this year, I was invited by the Government of the Republic of Korea and the Organization for Security and Co-operation in Europe (OSCE) Transnational Threats Department to address the 3rd Inter-Regional Conference on Cyber/ICT Security, on the issue of women in cyber policy. I stressed three points:

First, as we improve cybersecurity frameworks, we need to address the digital harm to women and girls. A good example of digital harm to women and girls is personal security and violence against women. Evidence shows

---

[9] Rebecca Oi, "Increasing Women's Representation in Cybersecurity," *Tech Wire Asia*, January 20, 2022, https://techwireasia.com/2022/01/increasing-women-representation-in-cybersecurity.

that with COVID-19 lockdowns, online misogynistic hate speech, revenge porn, deep fakes and the spread of misinformation have grown.

Second, with an increase in working from unsecure networks at home, there has been an increase in cybercrime. Amidst the pandemic, there has been a 600 per cent increase in malicious emails, with cyberattacks on information and communications technologies (ICTs) occurring every 39 seconds, and fake government websites designed to acquire individuals' personal information.[10] Criminal networks operating in the dark web, human traffickers and smuggling networks are taking advantage of the sudden and prolonged increase of women and girls online.

Third, there are several instruments and frameworks that policymakers can draw from when seeking to advance a gendered perspective within multilateral cybersecurity: UN Security Council Resolution 1325 on Women Peace and Security, Beijing Platform for Action and the Convention on the Elimination of All Forms of Discrimination Against Women (CEDAW). If more women are encouraged to understand cybersecurity, these instruments could be used to develop and strengthen gender-inclusive cybersecurity laws, policies and practices that respect the rights of women and girls and respond to their cybersecurity needs.

The UN considers Singapore to be an emerging "global leader in the field of cybersecurity" actively contributing to international, consensus-driven standards.[11] In 2020, Singapore and the UN agreed to develop a checklist with steps for countries to implement the 11 norms contained in the UN report on responsible state behaviour in cyberspace.[12] A gender analysis of these norms could provide guidelines for a more gender-aware

---

[10] "Top UN Official Warns Malicious Emails on Rise in Pandemic," *The Economic Times*, May 23, 2020, https://economictimes.indiatimes.com/news/international/world-news/top-un-official-warns-malicious-emails-on-rise-in-pandemic/articleshow/75914980.cms?from=mdr; "Hackers Attack Every 39 Seconds," *Security*, February 10, 2017, https://www.securitymagazine.com/articles/87787-hackers-attack-every-39-seconds.

[11] "Singapore to Work with UN to Help Nations Implement Norms for Responsible Cyber Behaviour," *The Straits Times*, November 2, 2020, https://www.straitstimes.com/tech/singapore-to-work-with-un-to-help-nations-implement-norms-for-responsible-cyber-behaviour.

[12] Tham Yuen-C, "Singapore, UN to Cooperate on Checklist for Countries to Implement Cyber-Security Norms," *The Straits Times*, October 9, 2020, https://www.straitstimes.com/singapore/politics/singapore-un-to-cooperate-on-checklist-for-countries-to-implement-cybersecurity.

approach to their implementation, and accelerate efforts to eliminate harassment and crimes in the cyber world. In so doing, Singapore could become not only a digital hub for global cybersecurity, but a digital hub with a human face.

Financial Hub for a Sustainable Future

How we deal with climate change and make the transition to a net-zero carbon society will define our future. ESG values are now becoming a prerequisite to create business value. It is about how successful businesses make their money, not about how they spend it once it is made. Successful businesses, in their enlightened self-interests, are changing their strategy to incorporate a triple bottom line to create both value and values to sustain their dynamism — people, planet, profit. According to a survey by Morgan Stanley, 90 per cent of millennial high net worth investors want to tailor their investments to their personal values, investing in companies with good ESG track records.[13] As a leading wealth management hub, Singapore can play a strong role in wealth planning solutions that support sustainable development in Asia.

Singapore has much at stake in global efforts to mitigate climate risk, and with the increasing threat of climate change, Singapore's sustainability agenda has taken on added urgency and broader dimensions. The country is actively developing strategies to reduce carbon emissions, becoming the first country in Southeast Asia to introduce a carbon tax. It is now positioning itself as a carbon services hub to complement Asia's decarbonisation efforts. There is good potential for Southeast Asia to generate carbon credits, and Singapore can play a role in the financing of projects that reduce or remove emissions through these credits. The immense financing needed to build a greener world can only be met through a combination of public and private capital. Singapore is also setting itself up as the leading centre for green

---

[13] "Morgan Stanley Survey Finds Investor Enthusiasm for Sustainable Investing at an All-Time High," *Morgan Stanley,* September 12, 2019, https://www.morganstanley.com/press-releases/morgan-stanley-survey-finds-investor-enthusiasm-for-sustainable-.

finance and markets, to facilitate Asia's transition to a sustainable future. It is promoting sustainability bonds and loans, and collaborating with international partners to develop a common green taxonomy. It is also building knowledge and capabilities in sustainable finance and has recently launched the Singapore Green Finance Centre. I was pleased to learn of these initiatives and more at the inaugural Singapore Sustainable Investing & Financing Conference organised by Temasek Holdings in partnership with BlackRock and the International Finance Corporation (IFC).

To ensure that all financial flows are consistent with a pathway towards low greenhouse gas emissions and climate resilient development, the UN Secretary-General has encouraged countries to set a carbon price, and has asked the Group of Twenty (G20) to consider the International Monetary Fund (IMF) proposal to create an international carbon price floor.[14] All financial actors must also set verifiable targets that cover their entire portfolios to shift them away from high-emission sectors to the climate resilient and net-zero economy, along with timelines to implement their pledges. Priority must be given to reducing carbon emissions across their entire value chain and holding to the highest standards of environmental integrity.

Conclusion

As we set our sights on the future, let us be mindful of the human condition and realities of our time. The political philosopher Hannah Arendt, writing after the devastation of World War II, offered her vision our future:

> *Never has our future been more unpredictable, never have we depended so much on political forces that cannot be trusted to follow the rules of common sense and self-interest — forces that look like sheer insanity, if judged by the standards of other centuries.*[15]

---

[14] Ian Parry, Simon Black, James Roaf, and IMF, "Proposal for an International Carbon Price Floor Among Large Emitters," *IMF Staff Climate Notes* 2021, no. 1 (June 2021).

[15] Hannah Arendt, "Preface to the First Edition," in *The Origins of Totalitarianism* (Cleveland: The World Publishing Company, 1958), vii.

As these lectures have shown, our world is now at a similar critical juncture, where we must act as a true global community for the sake of our collective future. Singapore must not only be part of this global community, we must also lead the way with sincerity and solidarity.

What type of nation can we become as we secure our future as a multilateral epicentre for the well-being of people and planet?

For me, Singapore can become a locally rooted nation with strong principles aligned with multilateral governance, a secure national core and increasingly comfortable with being a global citizen with the rights and responsibilities of what that entails. We could move from being identified as a little red dot to a beacon of smart and compassionate power, regionally and globally where our citizens can be counted on to revitalise multilateral governance. That is a future worth securing.

On Human Rights Day today (10 December), I would like to end my third lecture by returning to the beginning of our multilateral journey. Our forefathers and mothers vanquished the demons of the past, bequeathing to us a better world — and our generation was the main beneficiary. We are where we are today because of the foundation laid by the generation before us. In the words of Mahatma Gandhi: "The future depends on what you do today."

It is now our turn to fully comprehend and be a driving force to implement our common agenda, to rebuild multilateral governance. If we succeed it will be our turn to hear our children tell the story of how their parents' generation addressed the great disruptions, to heal the wounds of divisions, claim the storms of anger and secure the future where all children can flourish. I hope that these three lectures will ignite a national conversation towards envisioning a promising future — a future that celebrates the human spirit, where every person can live in freedom and dignity, where we can dare to imagine and co-create our communities, where our young can dream and awaken with the light of dawn shining in their eyes.

Question-and-Answer Session
Moderated by Professor Chan Heng Chee

Dr Noeleen Heyzer speaking with Professor Chan Heng Chee at her Q&A session
Source: Jacky Ho for the Institute of Policy Studies

Professor Chan Heng Chee: Noeleen, thank you very much for a very uplifting and wide-ranging speech. You have laid out very comprehensively the areas we have to address if we are going to secure our future, and to look at what a new multilateralism may look like. You've even touched on some areas for Singapore to take on if we want to be an epicentre of multilateralism. I'm a political scientist, so I would like to put in a reality check. I like your uplifting values and statements, but let me say this. I noticed you never mentioned the UN Security Council's five permanent members (P5), the big players, in your entire speech. I was in the UN from

1989 to 1991 and I saw how at the end of the Cold War, when the big powers stopped fighting each other and they could come together, how much could be done. Development, transnational issues, peacekeeping and so on. But now, the US and China's relationship is at its lowest point. How do you think we could attain your new multilateralism when two members of the P5, and perhaps more, are beginning to form alignments and coalitions? How do we progress forward?

Dr Noeleen Heyzer: First of all, Prof Chan, thank you so much for moderating this session. It's such an honour to have you with me this afternoon. You asked a very important question and indeed there was a time of great promise, especially after the end of the Cold War. In fact, there was a whole series of UN world conferences starting with the World Summit for Children in 1990. There were also conferences on the environment, on human rights, on population and so on. It was a time of great hope and great promise. But unfortunately, it did not last. And the reason why multilateral governance has been weakened is precisely because the superpowers cannot come together. Now the thing is, we can continue along that line but it's extremely dangerous. And I think if we want to have a stable world where people can function, independent of what their ideological or normative framework happens to be, the superpowers will have to find a way of working together. So I think we have to differentiate when the superpowers can come together and can cooperate. In fact, we have seen many attempts to at least cooperate in the area of the climate agenda, for example. Similarly, there are other areas where they can compete, and there's nothing wrong with healthy competition. But there are also other areas where there's huge contestation and they are never going to be able to agree.

I also don't think that the new multilateralism is solely dependent on the superpowers. This is because there is a diverse set of powers at play and even when, for example, under the previous regime when the US stepped out of the Paris Agreement, we still saw local governors and many corporations going ahead with it. So in a sense, power has become more diverse. It doesn't always have to be focused on the superpowers making a decision, and I think that provides a kind of space that is extremely helpful. So again, I think that we will have to navigate this. And I honestly think that because there are also coalitions of other member states, not just the superpowers, such as Singapore and its involvement with the Global Governance Group (3G) and Forum of Small States (FOSS). So, there are different spaces. It is not like the 20th century UN where everything was dependent on member states making decisions. Now, those who are willing to make decisions in different combinations would just go forward. That's my hopeful answer.

Prof Chan: Thank you, Noeleen. I'd like to take this a little further. Now, we do understand the Secretary-General is moving to the UN Summit of the Future and the Common Agenda. He is really trying to envision a UN 2.0 — a new multilateralism that is more inclusive and more networked. And being networked, you bring in more corporations, civil societies, individuals, young people, everyone. And I think we are moving in that way. But I also think that the UN is more suited to deal with issues of development and humanitarian crises than it is in dealing with peace and security. With peace and security, the big players are usually the ones who have disputes. This makes it very difficult for the UN. But, I believe the UN is very important and indispensable in peace and security type issues such as when dealing with women, children and refugees in war. I wonder if you agree with my very hard view of the work of the UN.

Dr Heyzer: Thank you, Prof Chan. The first thing that the Secretary-General did during his first term was to talk about prevention. He emphasised the need to have a prevention agenda because whatever it is or whoever starts the war, be it the big powers or whatever, nobody knows how to solve it. Today we have 84 million forcibly displaced people stuck with nowhere to go. Some wars have been going on forever and nobody knows how to solve these wars. But I don't think that if the UN is out that things will be better. In fact, it could even be worse.

What the Secretary-General has also done is to keep focusing on building an infrastructure of peace. I myself was involved with developing

UN Security Council Resolution 1325, and even at that time I spoke to the P5 and basically said, "Your approach to peace and security unfortunately is just a military approach. There are different perspectives emerging that need to be taken into account. You do not have an inclusive peace process." Because when we look at the countries that come back regularly onto the Security Council Agenda every five years, even after they think they have sorted a problem, conflict reappears again. And that's because the foundation of peace has not been built and the foundation of peace, unfortunately, involves the need to look at the root causes of conflicts, and these root causes very often are economic and social — it's political exclusion, it's governance issues, it's corruption, it's the breakdown of trust. There's no solidarity, it's a tearing of the social fabric. So as long as you have that, no one, including the superpowers, will be able to properly address sustaining peace and security. So this is a collective agenda, Prof Chan. It's a very serious agenda and I am absolutely concerned with the rate we are going, with the weapons that we have that are not under any regulatory framework. We have already seen this when civilian infrastructure, even hospitals, are bombed. There's no protection; the humanitarian law has been violated. So it's a very sad state and it is absolutely critical for the superpowers, and many of us, to come together and have this kind of conversation.

Prof Chan: I am fully in agreement with you; we are reaching a very critical stage. If we carry on this way, where would it lead us? You cannot solve violence, strife and war without addressing the root cause. I think that's why many leaders think the easiest way is to add more and more weapons which, as you point out, is not really the solution. The important question is, although we know what we have to do, how can we go about doing it and who should move it? Who moves to get things done? What coalitions should we build? I'm going to ask you a question from the audience, it's a bit of a deviation but important: What is your take on the decoupling of the US and China with the recent boycott of the Winter Olympics, how would it affect multilateralism? Is it going to be a drawback?

Dr Heyzer: I wouldn't say it's a multilateral issue if they boycott something. It is more of a bilateral issue. Nonetheless, I think that there are certain areas where there will be contestation between countries. Each country will need to decide how they want to deal with areas that they disagree. There are 193 countries in the UN, and multilateral governance involves having all countries coming together, being involved with global decision-making. And sometimes, especially in the UN, you are lucky if there is consensus. There are areas in which you will need to vote and then there are also areas where there are, I would say, innovative ways of addressing hard issues. So, I think the most important thing is that nobody wants to walk the road of breakdown. So eventually, everyone will have to manage their differences and take it very seriously because the threats are so real. If not, unfortunately, we may not survive if there is a third world war.

I think that there are enough very good people and enough wisdom to know how to manage differences. We are living in an extremely divided world, and I'm not surprised at the current tensions and divisions. But whatever it is, we have to find ways of not allowing the threads to just break apart. We have to make sure that the rope that's keeping us together does not unravel because it's going to be extremely hard to weave back the social fabric that has brought us here.

Prof Chan: Here's another question from the audience: You mentioned in your lecture the 12 areas of action that were identified by leaders in the UN Secretary-General report. One of these areas of action is to upgrade the UN. How do you think that would be achieved and how would an upgraded UN look like?

Dr Heyzer: It would be a more networked and inclusive UN. In fact, what the Secretary-General is doing now with the Summit of the Future is to get groups of former heads of states to work through some of these very critical issues and share their thoughts on what he has recommended. For example, he is thinking of turning the Trusteeship Council into a place where other stakeholders can come in, so that the youth, civil society and corporations can participate in it. So he is basically expanding on who would be involved with discussions on critical issues and organising things around key problems, and looking at who would have solutions and really going beyond just nation-states. Nation-states would play, as I mentioned in my speech, a very critical role because it gives authority — it provides the convening power, it gives legitimacy. But at the same time, I think our states are realising that they cannot do everything alone. Also, the fact that currently you have a dispersed network of power, even at the local and regional level, means that we are looking at new ways of solving problems.

Prof Chan: Thank you. We have another question from the audience.

Participant: Noeleen, I would like to ask you two bottom-line questions. Firstly, if you grabbed one of our 4G leaders, and he says, "I like what you're saying. But what should I do next?" What would your pithy pitch be? Secondly, if there are young people in the audience, if they say, "I want to give part of the next five years to helping the vision you're talking about to make Singapore an epicentre of multilateralism." What would or should this young person invest their time in?

Dr Heyzer: So, I was a bit brave to say that this is the Singapore that I would like to see. I'm actually quite proud of some of the things that I'm seeing, be it the social impact discussions in the country, especially during COVID-19. I find that people are becoming more caring, trying to find new ways of working, but there is always a "but" in what I'm going to say. The thing is all these are usually innovations. What I would like to see is that they become standard practice. Of course, there's a lot of encouragement for our youth to be innovative, to find solutions and create social impact. But at the same time, if it is to be practised, they have to partner with corporations, the government, and influence decision-making. It is not going to be easy. Already, corporations are struggling over what it means to be a net-zero carbon economy, what must change, how it would impact profits and so on. This is why I put out these ideas for national conversations. I hope that these lectures will make people excited to have conversations about what can be done and how can we do it.

One of my greatest hopes is that Singapore, whilst we're doing all these innovations internally, will also innovate externally. And there is so much need. I'm one of those people who have been working with the population that's been caught in precarious work for such a long time, the displaced population and so on. And you know, we are too small — at least this is the argument we have made — to get these people into our country. But they are in our neighbourhood and we have all the technology that can support their education and healthcare. So there are different ways in ASEAN where we can play a much stronger role — and with that education and mindset change — so that we are no longer a "little red dot". We can be a smart powerhouse that is also compassionate. I hope, and I know, that this is what we can be.

Prof Chan: I have to say, Noeleen, I absolutely agree that you have to keep the conversation going. For instance, the discussion on sustainability and climate change. Singapore is now talking about this all the time. Our politicians say that young people raise questions about climate change and worry about the environment. So, it is there and this is your new multilateralism. It's about people on the ground. And it could spread to other areas; it could be awareness about public health, rights to public health, global health and so on.

Dr Heyzer: Exactly.

Prof Chan: Now, I want to ask a question on the digital commons because this is very important and you spent a lot of time in your lecture talking about cybersecurity. The UN wants to reclaim the digital commons, and it's very good that you have established high-level cooperation on digital cooperation. There are talks and the UN is currently undertaking these talks. It is important because it may be the only platform that all the players are brought in. You can have digital agreements, economic agreements as groupings, but it's never totally inclusive. So where can you have a full discussion that includes everybody? I think the UN should keep doing that. I don't know what the play is like, and I should look into that how each player is pushing in cybersecurity. I'm sure many big players want to be the drivers, equal drivers, in forming digital rules. But my question is this: Do you think the UN should get a G20 Summit at the UN Headquarters so that you can discuss some of these issues? Because the G20 includes developed countries and developing countries, and most of the biggest players are there.

Dr Heyzer: Well you know, Heng Chee, one of the tracks for the Summit of the Future is on the global digital compact. And this is absolutely critical because a lot of the issues I mentioned in my lecture will be addressed and a regulatory framework will be discussed. The G20 members are part of this discussion as well. The UN is such a universal space to convene and in fact, there was already a High-Level Advisory Board on digital platforms that the Secretary-General organised. And actually, this would be a place to try out the new networked multilateralism, where we bring in the main players, because there's no point having just member states without the key players.

I know that Singapore has been very involved with the implementation of the 11 voluntary, non-binding norms on appropriate state behaviour in cyberspace, as recommended from the 2015 UN Group of Governmental Experts (UNGGE) report. It is critical, and people are looking at it more through a legal framework, and I just feel that there is a possibility for change. The UN has many weaknesses because it is in transition and it is never going to be perfect. But at the same time, I think the three roles that it plays make it so critical. First, the UN is a guardian of our future and it brings everybody together. It is a place where small states are represented and can network and create a much greater force. Second, it is a place to protect the international ethical framework because without that, we are going to be lost. And third, it is a convener and I feel that it provides legitimacy and authority for actions that are taken. Certain things become legal frameworks and international law, and we need that. As difficult as it is, we are there in the fight to secure a better future and we are walking hopefully along the road of breakthrough and not breakdown.

Prof Chan: And I hope the digital commons and the UN's attempts to create digital rules of the road will have the same sort of support and success even ground up from other sectors, as climate change has. I think everybody is interested in cybersecurity and cyber norms, and we're trying to come up with some rules. And I think this is where companies can all come in. On the issue of cybersecurity, you get all these major tech companies, whether it's Amazon or Microsoft, big e-commerce companies, major retailers and health companies; everyone is very concerned about cybersecurity and the protection of data. So you have already got them signing on. And in this new multilateralism, which you have emphasised, the UN is leading the way saying that "we want to have this discussion, we want the social compact, bring in the leaders, bring in the companies." In Singapore, we have to really make people more aware of the issue and the importance of cybersecurity, as well as the need to have talent, the people who can actually make this work. I hope this will grow because this is really a very important horizon for us.

Dr Heyzer: And also Prof Chan, this is an area where the young are far more advanced than many of us. And I would also like to see more women getting more engaged. I realised that when we hear of cybersecurity, we might think it's all about technology, but the banking group Citi basically convinced me that there's a whole range of skills and jobs available that they need women to be trained in. And I think that this is an area that I would encourage more women to get involved with, especially younger women.

Prof Chan: Thank you. Noeleen. We've now exceeded our time and I really want to thank you for a very interesting and inspiring presentation. We're always focused with the nitty-gritty of the facts, the realities. But we have to listen to values, we have to listen to what we should aim for, and I think you've done that greatly. And the UN is the place that we should go to and support, although sometimes we may wonder if the UN still relevant. I would say, though, that the UN is very relevant, particularly for the standard-setting and for looking at the many areas beyond peace and security that impinge on our lives. And I think you've drawn our attention very successfully to this in the last three lectures. Thank you very much. IPS is very lucky to have you as the 10th S R Nathan Fellow.

Dr Heyzer: Thank you very much, Prof Chan, and thank you all.

Bibliography

Akhmatova, Anna. "Requiem." In *Poems of Akhmatova*. Translated by Stanley Kunitz and Max Hayward. Boston: Houghton Mifflin, 1997.

Arendt, Hannah. "Preface to the First Edition." In *The Origins of Totalitarianism*, vii–ix. Cleveland: The World Publishing Company, 1958.

Asian Development Bank. "Key Indicators for Asia and the Pacific 2021." August 2021. https://www.adb.org/sites/default/files/publication/720461/ki2021.pdf.

Ban Ki-Moon. Opening Remarks at Press Encounter after Paris COP21 Conference, Paris, December 14, 2015. https://www.un.org/sg/en/content/sg/speeches/2015-12-14/opening-remarks-press-encounter.

Benjamin, Walter. "On the Concept of History (1940)." Translated by Dennis Redmond. Accessed December 20, 2021. https://www.marxists.org/reference/archive/benjamin/1940/history.htm.

Blue Planet II. Episode 7, "Our Blue Planet." Presented by David Attenborough. Aired December 10, 2017, on BBC. https://www.bbcearth.com/shows/blue-planet-ii.

Bunche, Ralph. "Some Reflections on Peace in Our Time." Nobel lecture delivered at the University of Oslo, December 11, 1950. https://www.nobelprize.org/prizes/peace/1950/bunche/lecture.

COP26 Coalition. "Global Day of Action for Climate Justice." https://cop26coalition.org/gda.

Credit Suisse. "Global Wealth Report 2021." June 2021. https://www.credit-suisse.com/about-us/en/reports-research/global-wealth-report.html.

Food and Agriculture Organization (FAO), UNICEF, World Food Programme (WFP) and World Health Organization (WHO). *Asia and the Pacific Regional Overview of Food Security and Nutrition 2020: Maternal and Child Diets at the Heart of Improving Nutrition*. Bangkok: FAO, 2021.

Forster, E M. "The Machine Stops." In *The Eternal Moment and Other Stories*, 3–37. United States: Harcourt Brace & Company, 1970.

Gafoor, Burhan. "Merits of Multilateralism." In *50 Years of Singapore and the United Nations*, edited by Tommy Koh, Li Lin Chang, and Joanna Koh, 78–84. Singapore: World Scientific, 2015.

Ghosh, Pallab. "Hawking Says Trump's Climate Stance Could Damage Earth." July 2, 2017. https://www.bbc.com/news/science-environment-40461726.

GlobalData. "Asia-Pacific Will Lead 5G Technology Adoption by 2024, Says GlobalData." January 13, 2020. https://www.globaldata.com/asia-pacific-will-lead-5g-technology-adoption-2024-says-globaldata.

"Hackers Attack Every 39 Seconds." *Security*, February 10, 2017. https://www.securitymagazine.com/articles/87787-hackers-attack-every-39-seconds.

Intergovernmental Panel on Climate Change (IPCC). "Climate Change Widespread, Rapid, and Intensifying." August 9, 2021. https://www.ipcc.ch/2021/08/09/ar6-wg1-20210809-pr.

International Fund for Agricultural Development. "2019 Rural Development Report: Creating Opportunities for Rural Youth." June 2019. https://www.ifad.org/documents/38714170/41133075/RDR_report.pdf/7282db66-2d67-b514-d004-5ec25d9729a0.

International Labour Organization (ILO). "Asia-Pacific Employment and Social Outlook 2020." December 15, 2020. https://www.ilo.org/wcmsp5/groups/public/---asia/---ro-bangkok/---sro-bangkok/documents/publication/wcms_764084.pdf.

Jessop, Simon, and Andrea Shalal. "COP26 Coalition Worth $130 Trillion Vows to Put Climate at Heart of Finance." *Reuters*, November 4, 2021, https://www.reuters.com/business/cop/wrapup-politicians-exit-cop26-130tn-worth-financiers-take-stage-2021-11-03.

Kierkegaard, Søren, "Journal JJ." In *Kierkegaard's Journals and Notebooks, Volume 2: Journals EE-KK*, 133–289. Princeton: Princeton University Press, 2008.

Kissinger, Henry. "Introduction." In *World Order: Reflections on the Character of Nations and the Course of History*, 1–7. London: Allen Lane/Penguin, 2014.

Koh, Tommy, Li Lin Chang, and Joanna Koh. "Preface." In *50 Years of Singapore and the United Nations*, edited by Tommy Koh, Li Lin Chang, and Joanna Koh, ix–xii. Singapore: World Scientific, 2015.

Lee, Hsien Loong. "Foreword." In *50 Years of Singapore and the United Nations*, edited by Tommy Koh, Li Lin Chang and Joanna Koh, v. Singapore: World Scientific, 2015.

Mahler, Daniel Gerszon, Nishant Yonzan, Christoph Lakner, R. Andres Castaneda Aguilar, and Haoyu Wu. "Updated Estimates of the Impact of COVID-19 on Global Poverty: Turning the Corner on the Pandemic in 2021?" *World Bank Blogs*, June 24, 2021. https://blogs.worldbank.org/opendata/updated-estimates-impact-covid-19-global-poverty-turning-corner-pandemic-2021?cid=SHR_BlogSiteShare_EN_EXT.

Ministry of Foreign Affairs (MFA). "MFA Press Statement: Caribbean Community (CARICOM) High-Level Ministerial Exchange Visit in Singapore 15 to 19 July 2013." July 15, 2013. https://www.mfa.gov.sg/Newsroom/Press-Statements-Transcripts-and-Photos/2013/07/MFA-Press-Statement-Caribbean-Community-CARICOM-HighLevel-Ministerial-Exchange-Visit_20130715.

———. "Speech by Minister for Foreign Affairs George Yeo at the 63rd Session of the United Nations General Assembly." September 29, 2008. https://www.mfa.gov.sg/Newsroom/Press-Statements-Transcripts-and-Photos/2008/09/Speech-by-Minister-for-Foreign-Affairs-George-Yeo-at-the-63rd-Session-of-the-United-Nations-General.

"Morgan Stanley Survey Finds Investor Enthusiasm for Sustainable Investing at an All-Time High." *Morgan Stanley*, September 12, 2019. https://www.morganstanley.com/press-releases/morgan-stanley-survey-finds-investor-enthusiasm-for-sustainable-.

National Archives of Singapore (NAS). "Statement of his Excellency S. Rajaratnam Foreign Minister of Singapore at the General Assembly on September 21 on the Occasion of Singapore's Admission to the United Nations," New York, September 21, 1965. https://www.nas.gov.sg/archivesonline/data/pdfdoc/PressR19650921.pdf.

Oi, Rebecca. "Increasing Women's Representation in Cybersecurity." *Tech Wire Asia*, January 20, 2022. https://techwireasia.com/2022/01/increasing-women-representation-in-cybersecurity.

Parry, Ian, Simon Black, James Roaf, and IMF. "Proposal for an International Carbon Price Floor among Large Emitters." *IMF Staff Climate Notes* 2021, no. 1 (June 2021).

Prime Minister's Office (PMO). "Intervention by PM Lee Hsien Loong at the APEC Informal Leaders' Retreat." July 16, 2021. https://www.pmo.gov.sg/Newsroom/PM-Lee-intervention-APEC-Informal-Leaders-Retreat-July-2021.

———. "Intervention by PM Lee Hsien Loong on 'Climate Change and Environment' at the G20 Rome Summit." October 31, 2021. https://www.pmo.gov.sg/Newsroom/Intervention-by-PM-Lee-Hsien-Loong-on-Climate-Change-and-Environment-at-the-G20-Rome-Summit.

———. "Intervention by PM Lee Hsien Loong on 'Global Economy and Global Health' at the G20 Rome Summit." October 30, 2021. https://www.pmo.gov.sg/Newsroom/Intervention-by-PM-Lee-Hsien-Loong-on-Global-Economy-and-Global-Health-at-the-G20-Rome-Summit.

———. "PM Lee Hsien Loong's Video Message at the Global Vaccine Summit." June 5, 2020. https://www.pmo.gov.sg/Newsroom/PM-Lee-Hsien-Loong-Global-Vaccine-Summit.

Reaching Everyone for Active Citizenry@Home (REACH). "Conversations on Singapore Women's Development." Accessed December 20, 2021. https://www.reach.gov.sg/Participate/conversations-on-singapore-womens-development.

Reuters. "World Has Entered Stage of 'Vaccine Apartheid' — WHO Head." May 17, 2021. https://www.reuters.com/business/healthcare-pharmaceuticals/world-has-entered-stage-vaccine-apartheid-who-head-2021-05-17.

Schneider Electric. "Building A Greener Singapore." October 12, 2021. https://www.se.com/sg/en/download/document/Building-a-Greener-SG_2021.

SDG Knowledge Hub, International Institute for Sustainable Development. "73 Countries Commit to Net Zero CO2 Emissions by 2050." December 17, 2019. https://sdg.iisd.org/news/73-countries-commit-to-net-zero-co2-emissions-by-2050.

"Singapore to Work with UN to Help Nations Implement Norms for Responsible Cyber Behaviour." *The Straits Times*, November 2, 2020. https://www.straitstimes.com/tech/singapore-to-work-with-un-to-help-nations-implement-norms-for-responsible-cyber-behaviour.

South African Government. "Statement of the President of the African National Congress, Nelson Mandela, at his Inauguration as President of the Democratic Republic of South Africa, Union Buildings, Pretoria." May 10, 1994. https://www.gov.za/statement-president-african-national-congress-nelson-mandela-his-inauguration-president-democratic.

Tham, Yuen-C. "Singapore, UN to Cooperate on Checklist for Countries to Implement Cyber-security Norms." *The Straits Times,* October 9, 2020. https://www.straitstimes.com/singapore/politics/singapore-un-to-cooperate-on-checklist-for-countries-to-implement-cybersecurity.

"Top UN Official Warns Malicious Emails on Rise in Pandemic." *The Economic Times*, May 23, 2020. https://economictimes.indiatimes.com/news/international/world-news/top-un-official-warns-malicious-emails-on-rise-in-pandemic/articleshow/75914980.cms?from=mdr.

Transform. "Our Portfolio." November 2020. https://www.transform.global/wp-content/uploads/2020/11/TRANSFORM-portfolio-overview-Nov20.pdf.

U Thant. *View from the UN*. Newton Abbot: David Charles, 1978.

United Nations (UN). "António Guterres: This is a Time for Science and Solidarity." April 14, 2020. https://www.un.org/en/un-coronavirus-communications-team/time-science-and-solidarity.

———. "IPCC Report: 'Code Red' for Human Driven Global Heating, Warns UN Chief." August 9, 2021. https://news.un.org/en/story/2021/08/1097362.

———. "New Global Deal that Shares Power, Resources Would be Crucial in Building Just, Sustainable Future, Secretary-General Tells World Summit for Social Development." December 1, 2020. https://www.un.org/press/en/2020/sgsm20465.doc.htm.

———. *Our Common Agenda — Report of the Secretary-General*. New York: United Nations, 2021.

———. "Secretary-General Calls Vaccine Equity Biggest Moral Test for Global Community, as Security Council Considers Equitable Availability of Doses." February 17, 2021. https://www.un.org/press/en/2021/sc14438.doc.htm.

———. "Universal Declaration of Human Rights." December 1948. https://www.un.org/en/about-us/universal-declaration-of-human-rights.

United Nations Development Programme (UNDP). *Human Development Report 1990: Concept and Measurement of Human Development*. New York: Oxford University Press, 1990.

United Nations Educational, Scientific and Cultural Organization (UNESCO). "UN Secretary-General Warns of Education Catastrophe, Pointing to UNESCO Estimate of 24 Million Learners at Risk of Dropping Out." August 4, 2020. https://en.unesco.org/news/secretary-general-warns-education-catastrophe-pointing-unesco-estimate-24-million-learners-risk.

United Nations Framework Convention on Climate Change (UNFCCC). "Secretary-General's Statement on the IPCC Working Group 1 Report on the Physical Science Basis of the Sixth Assessment." August 9, 2021. https://unfccc.int/news/secretary-general-s-statement-on-the-ipcc-working-group-1-report-on-the-physical-science-basis-of.

Woon, Wallace. "A Third of Businesses Here 'Strongly Aligned' with Singapore Green Plan 2030: Study." *The Straits Times*, October 12, 2021. https://www.straitstimes.com/singapore/environment/a-third-of-businesses-here-strongly-aligned-with-singapore-green-plan-2030.

Index

A

2030 Agenda for Sustainable Development, 11, 81
Access to COVID-19 Tools (ACT) Accelerator, 49
Access to COVID-19 Tools (ACT) Accelerator's Facilitation Council, 48
Africa, 38
African Union, 27
Agency for Integrated Care, 82
Albert Winsemius, 9
Amartya Sen, 11
Angel of History, 56, 65
Anna Akhmatova, 3
António Guterres, 2, 29, 36, 47, 51, 59, 71
artificial intelligence (AI), 38, 76
ASEAN Commission on the Promotion and Protection of the Rights of Women and Children (ACWC), 27
ASEAN Smart Cities Network (ASCN), 83
Asia, xi, xii, 3, 12, 13, 15, 16, 18, 38, 82, 83, 86, 87
Asian Miracle, 12, 13
Asia-Pacific, 13, 83, 84
Asia-Pacific Economic Cooperation Informal Leaders' Retreat, 48
Association of Southeast Asian Nations (ASEAN), 15, 18, 26–28, 52, 83, 95
Association of Southeast Asian Nations Charter, 26
Association of Southeast Asian Nations Community Vision 2025, 27
Association of Southeast Asian Nations Coordinating Centre for Humanitarian Assistance on Disaster Management (AHA), 26

B

Bangkok, 26
Bangladesh, 16
Ban Ki-Moon, 11
Beijing, 54
Beijing Platform for Action, 85
Berlin Wall, xi
BlackRock, 87
booster shots, 59, 62
breakdown, 21
breakthrough, 21, 22
Burhan Gafoor, 20
Burma, 7

C

Chew Tai Soo, 20
China, 15, 24, 29, 62, 90, 92
Citi, 83
civil society, 5, 17, 29, 30
climate action, 50
climate change, 38, 42, 46, 50, 54, 63, 66, 95, 97
climate crisis, xii, 36, 41, 50, 54, 58, 67

Coalition for Epidemic Preparedness Innovations (CEPI), 29, 48
Cold War, 6, 10, 11, 65, 90
Convention on the Elimination of All Forms of Discrimination Against Women (CEDAW), 27, 85
Copenhagen, 54
corporate governance, 15, 17, 22
corporate social responsibility (CSR), 17
COVID-19, xi, xii, 2, 13, 28, 39, 41, 42, 48–50, 58, 81, 85, 94
COVID-19 Vaccines Global Access (COVAX), 28, 29, 47–49
Credit Suisse, 14
Cuban Missile Crisis, 6
cyberattacks, 38
cybersecurity, 38, 42, 83–86, 95, 97

D
David Attenborough, x
decarbonisation, 52, 86
Declaration and Platform for Action, 55
Declaration on the Elimination of Violence Against Women, 30
democratic governance, 22
development, 5, 8–13, 15, 17, 18, 24, 27, 38, 40, 45, 47, 50, 51, 55, 66
digital commons, 73, 75, 95, 97
digital divide, 36, 42
digital literacy, 42

digital revolution, 38, 58, 67
displacement, 39, 50, 67
disruptions, 37
Dr Nafis Sadik, 55
Dr Tedros Adhanom Ghebreyesus, 47, 59, 62

E
Earth Summit, 11
education, 13, 18, 42, 55
E. M. Forster, 40
environment, social and governance (ESG), 18, 73, 74, 79, 86
equality, 44, 59
equal rights, 4, 7, 54
Europe, 3, 14, 38
European Union, 61

F
Factories Act, 18
Factory Asia, 15, 18
Forum of Small States (FOSS), 20, 31, 48, 65, 91
Fourth World Conference on Women, 11, 30

G
5G, 83
2008 Global Financial Crisis, xi
G20 Summit, 96
game changers, 46, 54–56
Gavi, the Vaccine Alliance, 29

gender equality, 45, 56, 59, 67
gender inequality, 54
George Yeo, 20, 31
global commons, 19, 22
Global Day of Action for Climate Justice, 54
Global Digital Compact, 76
global economy, 73
global governance, x, 40
Global Governance Group (3G), 31, 32, 46, 49, 50, 63, 91
global health governance, 47, 50
globalisation, x, 14
global public goods, 19, 22, 71, 73–78, 81
global public health, 41, 60, 81–83
Global Vaccine Summit 2020, 48
good governance, 12, 13, 43, 59, 67
Grace Fu, 53
gross domestic product (GDP), 14
gross national product (GNP), 11
Group of Twenty (G20), 29, 31, 49, 50, 52, 63, 87
Group of Twenty Summit, 49

H
Hannah Arendt, 87
healthcare, 18, 55, 81–83, 95
Helvi Sipilä, 55
Home Nursing Foundation, 82
human rights, xi, 4, 6, 11, 15–17, 24, 43, 44, 46, 59, 67, 72
Human Rights Day, 88

I
IBM, 83
inclusive society, 56
independence, 4, 5, 8, 9
inequality, 38, 41
inequalities, 42
information and communication technologies (ICT), 14, 42
intellectual property (IP), 60, 61
Intergovernmental Panel on Climate Change (IPCC), 51
international carbon price floor, 87
International Conference on Population and Development, 11
International Finance Corporation (IFC), 87
International Labour Organization (ILO), 17
International Labour Organization Declaration on Fundamental Principles and Rights at Work, 17
International Monetary Fund (IMF), 10, 11, 14, 87
Internet, 14
Internet of Things (IoT), 83, 84
Inter-Regional Conference on Cyber/ICT Security, 84

J
Janadas Devan, 23
Janet Lim, 67
Joe Biden, 62

K
Kofi Annan, 24
K. Shanmugam, 20

L
Lao People's Democratic Republic (PDR), 52
Lee Hsien Loong, 7, 48, 52
Lee Kuan Yew, 12
lifelong learning, 38
low-carbon solutions, 52

M
Mahatma Gandhi, 88
Mahbub ul Haq, 11
Mexico, 54, 55
Mia Amor Mottley, 31
Millennium Development Goals (MDGs), 11
mobile health (mHealth), 82
Moderna, 61
Morgan Stanley, 86
multilateral governance, xi, xii, 4–6, 9, 10, 19, 21, 22, 26, 28, 37, 43, 44, 46, 47, 51, 56, 71, 77–79, 88, 90, 93
multilateralism, x, xiii, 5, 12, 24, 26, 70, 71, 77, 78, 81, 89–92, 94, 95
multi-stakeholder alliances, 46

N
Nairobi, 54
nationalism, 46
Nationally Determined Contributions (NDCs), 52
Nelson Mandela, xiv
Netherlands, 9
net zero, 42, 50–52, 86, 87, 94
normative future, 54, 58

O
Omicron, 47
Operational Technology (OT), 83, 84
Organization for Security and Co-operation in Europe (OSCE), 84
Our Common Agenda, 21, 22, 57
Our Common Agenda report, 71, 72

P
Pakistan, 55
Paris Agreement, 51, 52, 90
Paris Climate Agreement, 11, 74
peace and security, xi, 5–7, 22, 25, 31, 36, 73, 74, 91, 92, 98
people-centred multilateralism, 5, 56
People's Democratic Republic (PDR)–Thailand–Malaysia–Singapore Power Integration Project (LTMS-PIP), 52
Pfizer, 61
populism, 44
poverty, 66
Powering Past Coal Alliance, 53

R
Ralph Bunche, 56
refugees, 39, 40, 82
renewed multilateralism, 57

Republic of Korea, 84
Rising Asia, 12, 13

S
2030 Sustainable Development Agenda, 27
Schneider Electric, 53
Security Council Resolution (SCR), 55
Singapore, xi–xiii, 37, 48, 52, 53, 56, 57, 59, 65, 67, 81–86, 88, 91, 94, 96, 97
Singapore core, 9
Singapore Green Finance Centre, 87
Singapore Green Plan 2030, 52, 53
Singapore Sustainable Investing & Financing Conference, 87
social contract, 71–73, 76
social inclusion, xi
social protection, 37, 39–41, 72
solidarity, 4, 19, 21, 22, 32
solidarity as self-interest, 19, 21, 31
Søren Kierkegaard, 70
South Asia, 80
Southeast Asia, 86
Soviet Union, 6
S. Rajaratnam, 8, 19, 31
St. Hilda Community Services, 82
Sub-Saharan Africa, 80
Summit of the Future, 76, 93, 96
Surin Pitsuwan, 27
sustainability, xi, 37, 38, 42, 45, 52, 59, 60, 72, 73, 86, 87, 95
sustainable, 49

Sustainable Development Goals (SDGs), 74
sustainable finance, 52
sustainable recovery, 37, 40, 41
Sweatshop Asia, 18

T
Temasek Holdings, 87
Tommy Koh, 7, 8, 26
TRANSFORM initiative, 80
trust, 64

U
2021 United Nations Climate Change Conference (COP26), 50, 53
UN Development Fund for Women (UNIFEM), 30
UN Framework Convention on Climate Change (UNFCCC), 51
UN Group of Governmental Experts (UNGGE), 96
United Kingdom's Foreign, Commonwealth and Development Office, 80
United Nations (UN), 2, 4, 6–11, 17, 20–31, 36, 37, 49, 51, 54, 55, 57, 65, 66, 71, 72, 76–79, 85, 87, 89, 91, 93, 96, 97
United Nations Charter, xi, 4–9, 11, 15, 26, 56, 77
United Nations Children's Fund (UNICEF), 9
United Nations Convention against Corruption, 17

United Nations Development Fund for Women (UNIFEM), 55
United Nations Development Programme (UNDP), 9, 11
United Nations General Assembly, 76
United Nations Global Compact, 17
United Nations Guiding Principles (UNGPs) for Business and Human Rights, 17
United Nations Industrial Development Organization (UNIDO), 9
United Nations International Children's Emergency Fund (UNICEF), 47
United Nations Population Fund (UNFPA), 55
United Nations Security Council, 5, 24, 29, 30, 49, 55
United Nations Universal Declaration of Human Rights, 17
United States (US), 4, 14, 29, 44, 62, 77, 90, 92
UN's 2030 Sustainable Development Agenda, 52
UN Secretary-General report, 93
UN Security Council Resolution 1325, 92
UN Security Council Resolution 1325 on Women Peace and Security, 85
UN Security Council's five permanent members (P5), 89, 92
UN Standards for Responsible Business and Human Rights, 17
UN Summit of the Future, 91
U Thant, 6, 7

V

vaccine multilateralism, 46–49
vaccines, 41, 46, 48–50, 59–61, 63

W

Winter Olympics, 92
women, 39, 45, 46, 54–56, 72, 75, 79, 80, 82, 84, 85, 97
Workplace Safety and Health Act, 18
World Bank, 9–11, 66
World Conference on Human Rights, 11
World Conference on Women, 55
World Health Organization (WHO), 29, 47, 49, 59
World Summit for Children, 90
World Summit for Social Development, 11
World Summit on Children, 11
World Trade Organization (WTO), 61
World War II (WWII), xi, 3, 4, 24–26, 36, 39, 87

Y

youth, 43, 44, 54, 94

www.ingramcontent.com/pod-product-compliance
Lightning Source LLC
Chambersburg PA
CBHW061943220426
43662CB00012B/2008